Asian Traditions and English Law
A Handbook

SEBASTIAN POULTER

The Runnymede Trust *with* **Trentham Books**

First published in 1990 by Trentham Books
Trentham Books
151 Etruria Road
Stoke-on-Trent
Staffordshire
England ST1 5NS

British Library Cataloguing in Publication Data
Poulter, Sebastian
   Asian traditions and English law: a handbook
   1. England. Law
   I. Title
   344.2

ISBN 0-948080-45-0

Typeset by The Design Bureau, Llay
Printed in Great Britain by BPCC Wheatons Ltd, Exeter

Asian Traditions and English Law
A Handbook

Contents

PREFACE

Many members of the various 'Asian' communities established in England today wish to preserve and maintain the traditions and customs which form an integral part of their cultural heritage. They are justly proud of these traditions, which are derived from ancient civilisations and deeply held religious beliefs.

However, living in England involves being subject to English law. This law, too, lays claim to a long history and it has its roots in the customs and values of the English people. It has grown up over many centuries through the decisions of the courts (the 'common law') and has been supplemented greatly in modern times by Acts of Parliament known as 'statutes' or 'legislation'.

To a large degree Asian traditions (in all their rich diversity) and English law are perfectly compatible with one another. English law generally favours individual freedom of action and allows people to do as they wish. As one judge succinctly stated in a case in 1979 —

> 'England, it may be said, is not a country where everything is forbidden except what is expressly permitted; it is a country where everything is permitted except where it is expressly forbidden.'

Naturally there are certain established ways of doing things, certain procedures to be followed if a person is always to be on the right side of English law and it is useful to know what these are. Moreover, sometimes there is a genuine 'clash of cultures' where a particular tradition comes into fundamental conflict with English values. Obvious examples include polygamy, forced marriages, female circumcision and certain types of Muslim divorce. However, the manner in which English law resolves these conflicts is often quite complex and requires careful examination.

The main aim of this handbook, the first of its kind to be published in Britain, is to act as a guide to the ways in which Asian traditions and the provisions of English law relate to one another. It is written in a style that is deliberately free

1

of legal jargon so that it can easily be read and understood by non-lawyers. It is hoped that it may prove useful to many individuals in the Asian communities who would like to learn more about what their legal rights and duties are in England and how far English law goes in respecting their cultural values and traditional practices. It should also be a valuable work for those who give advice and assistance in a variety of welfare agencies such as community organisations, citizens' advice bureaux, law centres, trade unions etc.

Of course, in a short book of this nature it is impossible to give all the details of English law on each subject examined. A more wide-ranging and comprehensive treatment of many of the topics dealt with here is available in my earlier study entitled *English Law and Ethnic Minority Customs* (Butterworths, 1986). In any event, where a person has a really difficult legal problem which needs to be resolved through court proceedings, practical legal advice and assistance should obviously be sought from a solicitor.

Over seventy cases decided by the English courts are mentioned in the book. They are used both to illustrate the principles being expounded and because they stand as authorities ('precedents') in the English legal system in their own right and hence may well be relied upon by judges in future cases. The full reference to every case in the law reports is given at the end of the book so that legal practitioners can quickly identify and locate them when advising clients. A case usually begins in a magistrates' court, a Crown court or a county court though the more important cases often start in the High Court. Appeals can be made to the Court of Appeal and in a few cases a further appeal is possible to the highest court in the land, the House of Lords. The higher the court in which a decision is reached, the greater its importance ranks as a 'precedent'.

In some fields it is well known that members of Asian communities prefer, where possible, to settle disputes and compromise claims without involving the English courts in what might be regarded as a community or family matter. English law has no objection such systems of extra-judicial mediation, conciliation or arbitration, but it may nevertheless be useful for those negotiating or deciding upon such settlements to know what English law provides in such circumstances.

Whatever your interest may be in this subject, whether to try to sort out your own legal problems or those of others, or simply an intellectual curiosity about how English law and Asian traditions interact, it is hoped that this handbook will help to clarify the situation for you.

The credit for transforming my untidy manuscript into a suitable typescript for the publishers belongs to Margaret Newton and Ingrid Butcher, to whom I should like to express my sincere thanks.

Sebastian Poulter

CHAPTER 1

Introduction

Although there are no reliable official statistics about the ethnic origins of the population of Great Britain at the present time, it is widely believed that the number of 'Asians' or people who would describe their ethnic origins as 'Asian' exceeds 1.5 million. Most of them or their parents have come directly from the South Asian countries of India, Pakistan, Bangladesh and Sri Lanka. Others arrived via the East African states of Kenya, Uganda, Tanzania and Malawi, to which sizeable numbers of people from the Indian subcontinent emigrated during the colonial period. There are also over 120,000 Chinese living in England today as well as smaller numbers of Vietnamese, Arabs and Iranians (amongst others). Some Asians now regard England as their permanent home while others view their stay in this country as merely temporary and intend ultimately to return to their countries of origin.

Residence and Domicile

Of those Asians who are resident in England, by no means all are 'domiciled' here. Domicile is a technical legal expression of considerable importance in many areas and its meaning needs to be clarified at the outset. A person is treated as domiciled in the country or legal jurisdiction which is regarded as his or her 'real home' or 'permanent base'. Children under the age of 16 cannot decide upon their own domiciles — they automatically take on those of their parents and at birth they acquire a 'domicile of origin'. However, from the age of 16 everyone is free to alter their inherited domicile and acquire a new 'domicile of choice'. This is done by forming an intention to reside permanently (rather than merely temporarily) in the country in which they are living. A few examples may help to illustrate the point.

3

- Mr. Patel came to England from India in 1964 and was later joined here by other members of his family. He always intended to return to India when he had saved enough money for his retirement. He has invested in property in India over the past 15 years and still has every intention of eventually returning there for good. He has clearly retained his Indian domicile throughout and has not acquired an English 'domicile of choice'. However, his children, who are now in their thirties and obtained most of their schooling here, have decided they wish to remain in England permanently. Although they inherited their father's Indian domicile as their 'domicile of origin' they have changed over to an English 'domicile of choice' through their intention, formed after the age of 16, to stay here and regard England as their permanent base. This will not be affected by the fact that they make frequent visits to India to see relations etc.

- Mr. Singh was forced to flee from Uganda in 1968 as a result of persecution by Idi Amin. He held a British passport and soon after arriving in England he made the decision to remain here and rebuild his life here. He therefore acquired an English domicile as from that time.

- Miss Wong came to England from Hong Kong last year to study for a degree. Since she intends to return to Hong Kong at the end of her course she does not possess an English domicile. However, if at the conclusion of her course she is allowed to stay in Britain (e.g. she marries a person with an English domicile or she obtains long-term employment here) she may eventually decide to stay on permanently, with the result that she becomes domiciled here.

Do wives automatically have the same domiciles as their husbands?

Under English law they used to, but not any longer (Domicile and Matrimonial Proceedings Act 1973). However, in practice the domiciles of husbands and their wives will usually be the same if they are living together in the same country. On the other hand, if a man has come to England to make a new life and has decided to abandon his wife whom he has left behind in the Indian subcontinent, the couple's respective domiciles will obviously be different.

Does citizenship or nationality affect domicile?

The two concepts do not necessarily correspond because citizenship and nationality are matters of a person's political status and allegiance, whereas domicile relates to questions of civil status (e.g. in family law issues). However, if a man has acquired British nationality by the voluntary process of becoming naturalised it may well indicate that his intention was to make his permanent home here. However, he may later decide otherwise and he is perfectly free to acquire a new domicile if he so wishes, despite retaining British nationality. He might, for example, have come to Britain from Iran after the fall of the Shah, have become a naturalised British subject and, having recently spent a year in Toronto, decide that he wishes to make his permanent home in Canada. If he takes up permanent residence in Canada he will become domiciled there, regardless of his British citizenship.

How is a person's domicile actually proved?

Although, as we have seen, the domicile of anyone over the age of 16 rests largely on that person's intentions as to his or her permanent home, the matter is sometimes controversial. A person's claim to be domiciled in a particular country at a particular time may be challenged in a court case or disputed by an official in a government department. Evidence of such intention will then need to be given, displaying strong links with the country concerned in the form of, for example, a house there, employment, investment, periods of residence, frequency of visits, family and friends and business contacts etc. No single type of link — or its absence — will be decisive or conclusive; the question is ultimately whether a convincing argument can be made for a person's 'real home' being where it is claimed to be.

In one case the individual's 'tastes, habits, conduct, actions, ambitions, health, hopes and projects' were all held by the judge to be relevant factors to be taken into account. In another case, *Qureshi v. Qureshi* (1972), it was stated that there was a presumption against the acquisition by someone of a domicile of choice in a country whose religion, manners and customs differed widely from those of his domicile of origin. However, this presumption may easily be disproved and obviously many people from Asian countries are now domiciled in England. It is worth noting that no-one can acquire a domicile of choice in a country in which he is residing illegally, in violation of the immigration laws.

Can a person have a 'British' domicile?

The answer is 'no'. This is because a person has to have a domicile in a country with a separate legal system. Since England, Scotland and Northern Ireland, for example, all have distinctive legal systems, a person can only be domiciled in one of these — not in Britain as a whole. Moreover, no-one can be domiciled in two countries at the same time, despite having strong connections with each country. Only one will be treated, in legal terms, as a person's domicile, namely the one in which that person is regarded as having his or her permanent home.

CHAPTER 2

Getting married in England

When an Asian couple get married in England, both they and their families will usually wish to follow the traditions and customs appropriate to their religious and cultural backgrounds. However, the rules of English law need to be followed as well, if the marriage is to be treated as legally valid.

1   FORMALITIES

Save in the exceptional case of a Church of England wedding (which is normally preceded by the 'calling of banns') the parties must usually first obtain a Superintendent Registrar's 'Certificate', or 'Certificate and Licence'. The latter documents combined cost more than the Certificate on its own, but their possession enables a couple to marry more quickly and with less publicity — which are sometimes seen as advantages by the couple themselves, if not by their two families.

Advance notice of the wish to marry needs to be given to the Superintendent Registrar before either the 'Certificate' or the 'Certificate and Licence' can be issued. In order to obtain a 'Certificate' the notice has to be given to the Superintendent Registrar of the district or districts where the parties have been living for the previous seven days, whereas in the case of a 'Certificate and Licence' the notice only has to be given to the Superintendent Registrar of the district where one of them has resided for the previous fifteen days. Where the notice is given by someone who appears to be of foreign origin, some Superintendent Registrars have adopted the practice of asking to see their passports, both to check that they have been resident locally for the required period and to ensure that they are above the minimum age for marriage (as to which see page

10). There is no legal right to insist upon the production of a passport before issuing a 'Certificate' or a 'Certificate and Licence', but in the case of *Tejani v Superintendent Registrar for the District of Peterborough* (1986) the Court of Appeal decided that to ask for a passport to be shown in these circumstances was not a contravention of the Race Relations Act 1976. Mr Tejani was a British citizen who had been born in Uganda and who had been living in England for 12 years before he visited his local Superintendent Registrar with a view to giving notice of his plan to marry in Peterborough. He was obviously very surprised to be asked to show his passport and therefore brought legal proceedings against the Superintendent Registrar, but the Court's decision makes it clear that such requests are not illegal. On the other hand, there is no need to produce a passport if residence within the district can be proved in some other way.

Where can a marriage ceremony take place?

The basic choice is usually between a Register Office and a religious building, ie one which has both been certified by law as a place of religious worship and been registered by the Registrar-General for use in the solemnisation of marriages (Marriage Act 1949). Mosques, Hindu and Buddhist temples and Sikh *gurdwaras* may all be certified and registered if the appropriate conditions are satisfied, but many such buildings have not in fact been certified and registered and it is therefore advisable for the couple to check up on this point when the wedding details are being arranged. One explanation for this situation is that only 'separate' buildings can be certified and registered, which means that the whole building has to be used as a place of worship, whereas most mosques, *gurdwaras* and temples are either treated as community centres (where a great variety of social activities are carried on) or else they are simply rooms in ordinary private residential accommodation. If the local mosque, temple or *gurdwara* has not been registered for marriages, the couple can go through the common procedure of first attending a civil ceremony at a Register Office (the real marriage in the eyes of the English law but often no more than a betrothal in the minds of the participants) and, if they wish, subsequently having a religious wedding at the place of worship (often the real marriage in the eyes of the couple and their community).

Who conducts the wedding ceremony?

The Superintendent Registrar officiates, together with a Registrar, at marriages in a Register Office, while a minister of the religion concerned usually conducts a wedding in a registered building. The minister does not have to possess any particular qualifications; he merely needs the authorisation of the trustees or governing body of the building and the Registrar-General and Superintendent Registrar of the district should both be notified of the authorisation given.

Who decides what form the ceremony takes?

Register Office weddings must be purely secular (non-religious) in form, whereas those in a registered building may follow whatever lines the parties and those in charge of the building feel is suitable. However, in both types of ceremony the parties must, with the doors open and in the presence of at least two witnesses, first declare that they know of no lawful impediment (obstruction) to the marriage and then exchange formal vows that they are taking one another as husband and wife (Marriage Act 1949). This means that the parties must attend the ceremony in person and that proxies (agents) are not allowed. Although in Muslim law a marriage can be contracted by representatives of the couple who have been duly authorised to act as agents on their behalf, such a procedure would not result in a valid marriage in English law even if the mosque in which it occurred had been registered by the Registrar-General.

2 CAPACITY TO MARRY

Apart from insisting that spouses should be of the opposite sex, English law has various rules about who may validly marry whom. Certain close relatives cannot marry one another because they fall within the prohibited degrees (e.g. a man cannot marry his mother, daughter, grandmother, grand-daughter, sister, aunt or niece). A minimum age is laid down and bigamy and polygamy are outlawed. A party may escape from a marriage to which he or she has not properly consented. These points are explored further below.

Can cousins marry one another in England?

Yes, there is no restriction upon such marriages whatever. There have, however, been some reports of the children of Muslim cousin marriages in England being born handicapped because of the recessive genes of their parents and it would therefore seem sensible for anyone contemplating such a marriage to take medical advice. Genetic counselling is now widely available within the National Health Service and can help in identifying the risks involved.

Is there any barrier to marrying out of one's religion or caste?

No such barrier exists under English law. A marriage between a Muslim woman and a non-Muslim man, though not permitted in Islamic law, would be recognised as valid here. Similarly a marriage between a *brahmin* and a *shudra* or between a Sikh and a Christian would be perfectly lawful. In this respect it does not make any difference whether the parties are domiciled in England or abroad.

What is the minimum age for getting married?

No-one can marry under the age of 16, even if their religion allows it. Any such attempted marriage will be invalid or 'void' (Matrimonial Causes Act 1973). A person who wishes to marry between the ages of 16 and 18 requires parental consent, although if such consent is not obtained the marriage will still be valid.

Can a Muslim who already has a wife in the Indian subcontinent marry another wife in England?

Not until he has obtained a recognised divorce from his first wife. No-one can validly marry in England while still married to someone else (Matrimonial Causes Act 1973). The second attempted marriage is invalid and there may also be a prosecution for the crime of bigamy. Muslims are not permitted actually to practise polygamy through a marriage entered into in this country.

Are arranged marriages accepted by English law?

The normal pattern of an arranged marriage, in terms of which the choice of partners is made by the parents (or other relatives of the spouses) and this is agreed to by the spouses themselves, is perfectly acceptable in law. The spouses will have been brought up to believe that their parents have the right to make this choice, that they have their children's long-term welfare at heart and that they will choose wisely. They may therefore willingly assent to the marriage, no doubt with a greater or lesser degree of enthusiasm, depending upon their personalities and the impression made upon them by their partner during the limited opportunities the couple will have had to get to know one another before the wedding. However, where the parents propose a spouse who is totally unacceptable to their son or daughter, the marriage should not proceed and a new bride or bridegroom will have to be found.

But surely there are some cases where young people have been forced into marriages against their wishes?

Indeed there are and English law does not approve of these marriages. A person who has not properly consented to the marriage because his or her wishes have been overridden by pressure or threats, can petition (apply to) the court to have the marriage set aside and nullified (Matrimonial Causes Act 1973). The marriage is regarded in legal terms as 'voidable', ie capable of being avoided. It is necessary for legal proceedings to be taken, within 3 years of the wedding, in order to obtain a decree of annulment from the court. In the case of *Hirani v. Hirani* (1983) an Indian Hindu girl of 19 had made her parents angry by forming an association with a Muslim man. Her parents soon made arrangements for her to marry a Hindu instead, choosing a man neither they nor their daughter had ever met. They put pressure on her by threatening to throw her out of the family home if she refused to go ahead with the wedding. In the end she went through both a civil marriage in a Register Office and a religious ceremony six weeks later. She cried throughout the religious ceremony and was utterly miserable. Later she went to live with her husband for a short time, but the marriage was never consummated by sexual intercourse. She succeeded in her petition to the Court and her marriage was annulled. This meant she was free to marry someone else without having to get divorced. By no means all the petitions for annulment of marriage brought by young Asians on grounds of lack of consent have been successful. Important factors include the state of mind of the petitioner, the weakness of his or her position vis-a-vis those who are arranging the marriage (including age and sex), whether he or she had an opportunity to meet the other spouse prior to the wedding, the degree of pressure exerted by the family and the alternative courses of action open to the petitioner. Ultimately it is for the English court to decide whether there was lack of consent to the marriage as a result of what the law describes as 'duress'. In the case of *Singh v. Singh* (1972) the Court of Appeal adopted a very hard line in refusing to annul the marriage of a 17 year old Sikh girl, insisting that she needed to prove that she was in fear of imminent danger in order to satisfy the test of 'duress'. However, it seems unlikely that future courts will take such a tough stand on the question.

Are there any other significant grounds upon which a marriage is voidable?

Another situation where a marriage is 'voidable' is where one spouse is either incapable of consummating the marriage (ie unable to have normal sexual relations with the other spouse) or is wilfully refusing to commence such relations when perfectly capable of doing so. With respect to the latter ground, a spouse who has a good reason for refusing to begin sexual relations is not considered to be acting 'wilfully'. An example will make this clearer. In the case of *Kaur v. Singh* (1972) a Sikh couple had gone through a Register Office marriage but had not yet had the religious wedding. The wife would naturally have refused to have sexual intercourse with the husband until after the religious wedding but the husband would not have anything to do with the proposed religious ceremony. The Court decided that the husband was really the one who was acting 'wilfully' in refusing to consummate the marriage in that he was

11

refusing to co-operate in going through what was, in terms of the couple's religious beliefs, a pre-condition to the commencement of sexual relations between them. The wife was therefore granted a decree of annulment.

A Muslim wife whose husband fails to pay her the dower (*mahr*) due to her on marriage would probably also have a good legal reason for refusing to consummate the marriage and so not be acting 'wilfully'. She could successfully petition for annulment herself because it would really be her husband who was refusing to co-operate in completing the true marriage between them. *Mahr* is discussed further in chapter 8.

CHAPTER 3

Getting married overseas

A couple who are validly married in one country may not necessarily be regarded as married by the law of another country. This chapter considers the various ways in which English law examines a foreign marriage in order to decide whether or not to recognise its validity. Some of the important consequences of its acceptance as a valid marriage are described in chapter 5.

The fundamental principle of English law is that a foreign marriage will be treated as valid here, provided that —

(a) it complied with the 'formalities' laid down by the law of the country where it was contracted;

and

(b) the parties had the necessary 'capacity to marry' in terms of the laws of their respective domiciles (for the meaning of 'domicile' see above, pages 3-5).

'Formalities' relate to matters such as where a couple may get married (type of building), the form the ceremony must take (religious or secular), how many witnesses should be present, etc. In these respects the law of the country where the ceremony took place must have been properly followed. So far as questions of 'capacity to marry' are concerned, the two principal areas of practical importance relate to minimum age and polygamy. In each case the laws of the couple's domiciles must have been complied with, if the marriage is to be regarded as valid in England. Some examples will hopefully clarify the position.

1 MINIMUM AGE

- A Muslim marriage is contracted in one of the states bordering the Arabian Gulf by a couple who are each domiciled there. The bride is only 13 years old, but this is permissible under the state's own law (which follows Islamic principles, in terms of which girls may marry from puberty onwards). The marriage would be recognised as valid in the eyes of English law. However, as a result of a clause in the Immigration Rules introduced in 1986, the wife would not be allowed to enter the UK in her capacity as a spouse until she attained the age of 16, the minimum age for getting married in England. Hence she could not, for example, accompany her husband if he came for a course of study in the UK, until she reached 16.

- An Asian girl of 15 who has an English domicile of origin (derived from her father's decision to make his permanent home in England) goes to India and enters into a marriage there with an Indian man. Although the marriage may be valid in India it will be invalid in English law because 16 is the minimum age for marriage for those domiciled in England. They do not have the legal capacity to get married abroad under that age. The man will not be allowed to enter the UK as the girl's 'husband', even after she reaches 16.

- A Bangladeshi man of 23 who has a domicile of choice in England, returns to Bangladesh to marry a girl of 14 who is domiciled there. The marriage may be valid in Bangladesh but it will not be treated as a marriage in English eyes because a person domiciled in England does not have the capacity to enter into a marriage with a person under 16.

Note: In each of the last two examples the underlying purpose of English law is to protect people who are domiciled in England from entering into a youthful marriage which may later break down through the immaturity of one or both of the partners. In the Indian subcontinent the same objective is pursued by laws which impose criminal penalties upon those who marry girls under 16 (in Pakistan and Bangladesh) or under 18 (in India), though the actual marriages are treated as valid.

2 POLYGAMY

If two people, both of whom are domiciled in countries or jurisdictions where polygamy is permitted, contract a marriage under a polygamous system then their marriage will be treated as valid in the eyes of English law. This is so, regardless of whether the husband is already married to someone else (in which case it will be an 'actually polygamous ' marriage) or was a bachelor prior to the wedding (in which case it will merely be a 'potentially polygamous' marriage in terms of which he may later marry other wives if he so wishes). This assumes, of course, that the normal system of polygamy (many wives) applies, rather than the far rarer system of polyandry (many husbands). It is possible that there is an exception to the above rule where the husband was a party to a subsisting prior marriage which had been entered into *in England*, but the question has not yet been decided by the English courts. If such an exception did exist in these circumstances then the second marriage would be invalid in the eyes of English law.

Is the position the same if the husband is domiciled in England?

It used to be thought that a foreign polygamous marriage would never be valid in English law in such circumstances because of a provision in the Matrimonial Causes Act 1973, but the case of *Hussain v. Hussain* (1983) establishes that while an actually polygamous marriage will always be invalid, a marriage which is the husband's only one at the time (ie merely potentially polygamous) will be recognised as valid in English law. In that case the couple, who were both Muslims, had gone through an Islamic ceremony of marriage in Pakistan at a time when the husband was domiciled in England and the wife was domiciled in Pakistan. The English Court was required to decide whether the marriage was valid, bearing in mind the fact that under the law of Pakistan the husband would be entitled to marry further wives. The Court indicated that since under English law the husband was barred from taking any further wives because of his English domicile, his marriage was really a monogamous one (whatever view the law of Pakistan might take of the position) and hence valid in England. However, the Court did acknowledge that there was an inconsistency in English law here because such a marriage would not have been valid if the domiciles of the husband and wife had been the other way round. If the wife had been domiciled in England and the husband domiciled in Pakistan, the husband would have been allowed by the law of his country of domicile (Pakistan) to become a polygamist. Hence the marriage would have been invalid here because the wife would have possessed an English domicile and would have been attempting to enter into a potentially polygamous marriage, which English law forbids.

Can a husband who is validly married to two or more wives bring each of them to the UK to settle here with him?

This practice has recently been restricted by provisions in the Immigration Act 1988 and changes in the Immigration Rules which came into force on 1st August

15

1988. A wife who is a party to an actually polygamous marriage and who has not been in the UK for the purpose of settling here, on the basis of her marriage, before 1st August 1988, will not now be allowed to enter for settlement at any time in the future, if another of her husband's wives (or widows) has preceded her in settling in the UK or in being granted entry clearance to come here to settle. It should be noted that no special preference is given under the Act to the first wife in a polygamous marriage. Hence if the second wife comes to settle in the UK, this will prevent the first wife later coming to settle. The new rules only affect those who apply to enter the UK after 1st August 1988 and thus wives of a polygamous husband who were settled here before that date are not affected by the new provisions and are entitled to remain in the UK. Moreover, the provision does not bar short visits of up to six months from wives who are covered by the new law; they are simply prevented from being able to stay here indefinitely for purposes of settlement. The basic idea behind the provision seems to be to prevent a husband simultaneously having two or more wives living with him in the UK, on the grounds that polygamy is not in keeping with British social values. However, the new law is very widely drafted and is capable of barring a second wife in a polygamous marriage from entry to the UK even after the first wife's death.

CHAPTER 4

Arranged marriages and British immigration law

For a number of years, successive British governments have tried to devise ways of preventing people migrating permanently to the UK on the basis of bogus 'marriages of convenience'. Equally undesirable are forced marriages in which Asian girls living in Britain are pressurised into marrying men from the Indian subcontinent so that their husbands can settle in the UK. The problem has been how to frame rules which are effective in prohibiting these rather distasteful practices, without at the same time restricting the entry of genuine spouses who are parties to an arranged marriage. It is a regrettable fact that the current Immigration Rules undoubtedly do have an adverse impact on arranged marriages and the details of the law require careful explanation.

There are separate, though similar, rules for those who seek admission to the UK as existing spouses of persons 'settled' in the UK and those who apply to enter in order to marry someone 'settled' in the UK (ie a fiancé or a fiancée). A person is 'settled' in the UK if he or she ordinarily lives here and no time limit on staying in the UK has been imposed by the immigration authorities. However, both categories of applicant are required to hold entry clearance certificates. These certificates will be refused by the entry clearance officer unless the officer is satisfied that the following conditions are met —

(a) **In the case of fiancés or fiancées —**

(i)   that it is not the primary purpose of the intended marriage to obtain admission to the UK; and

17

(ii)   that there is an intention that the parties to the marriage should live together permanently as husband and wife; and

(iii) that the parties to the proposed marriage have met; and

(iv)   that adequate maintenance and accommodation, without recourse to public funds, will be available for the applicant until the date of the marriage; and

(v)   that there will thereafter be adequate accommodation for the parties and their dependants, without recourse to public funds, in accommodation of their own or which they occupy themselves; and

(vi)   that the parties will thereafter be able to maintain themselves and their dependants adequately without recourse to public funds.

(b) In the case of spouses —

(i)   that the marriage was not entered into primarily to obtain   admission to the UK; and

(ii)   that each of the parties has the intention of living permanently with the other as his or her spouse; and

(iii) that the parties to the marriage have met; and

(iv)   that there will be adequate accommodation for the parties and their dependants, without recourse to public funds, in accommodation of their own or which they occupy themselves; and

(v)   that the parties will be able to maintain themselves and their dependants without recourse to public funds.

How does one decide whether the primary purpose of a marriage is to gain entry to the UK?

If an applicant is dissatisfied with the decision of an entry clearance officer, he or she can appeal first to an Immigration Adjudicator, then to the Immigration Appeal Tribunal and ultimately in an appropriate case to the High Court, Court of Appeal and House of Lords. In a number of court cases the judges have attempted to clarify how the 'primary purpose' rule should be interpreted and applied.

In *R v Immigration Appeal Tribunal, ex parte Bhatia* (1985) the applicant Vinod Bhatia, an Indian citizen, had applied in 1981 for an entry clearance certificate in New Delhi to enable him to come and marry Vijay Kumari in England and settle here. She was already settled in the UK, having arrived in 1970 and been married and divorced here. She had a ten year old child from her first marriage. Vijay's parents placed an advertisement in the *Hindustan*

Times in India seeking a second husband for her, not an easy task with respect to a Hindu woman who has been divorced. Bhatia responded to the advertisement and was considered suitable by Vijay's parents. She met him in New Delhi in 1980 while she was there for the wedding of her sister. The marriage was arranged but the immigration officer, who subsequently interviewed Bhatia, refused to give him an entry clearance certificate to come to England because he was not satisfied that it was not the primary purpose of the intended marriage to obtain his admission to the UK. Bhatia made a number of appeals but these were all rejected, the final decision being made by the Court of Appeal. Certain key principles emerge from the Court's ruling in this case. First, it is for the applicant to prove, on a balance of probability, that the primary purpose of the intended marriage was not entry to the UK. Secondly, the fact that the applicant can prove the marriage to be a genuine one, as opposed to a mere sham 'marriage of convenience', is not enough. The primary reason behind it could still be found to be entry to the UK, as in this case. Here there was no doubt in the Court's mind that Bhatia and Vijay genuinely intended to enter into a real marriage and live together. Thirdly, it is perfectly proper for the immigration officer to bear in mind the intentions and purposes stated by the couple's parents and other family members as being their reasons for arranging a particular marriage. In this case, while Vijay and her parents clearly wanted her marriage to Bhatia in order to get her a second husband in her difficult circumstances as a divorcee with a child, Bhatia told the immigration officer that he did not think his father would have agreed to the marriage had Vijay not been settled in England. Hence Bhatia's father's primary purpose, and by implication Bhatia's own primary intention too, was that the marriage would gain him entry to the UK.

Two useful lines of argument to prove that a marriage was not being entered into primarily for immigration purposes are illustrated by another case, *R v Immigration Appeal Tribunal, ex parte Kumar* (1986). Here the applicant Arun Kumar, an Indian Hindu, applied for an entry clearance certificate not as a fiancé (as in *Bhatia's* case) but as a husband. He had married Santosh Kumari, a British citizen who was born in the UK. It seemed to be part of a system of interlocking marriages between the two families, for his elder brother was already married to an aunt of his wife. If a pattern of interconnected family unions can be demonstrated, this may help to indicate what the primary purpose of the marriage really was. However, the more crucial fact in this case was that after the marriage between Kumar and Santosh had taken place in the Punjab in 1982, the couple lived in Kumar's father's house in India for over a year before Santosh returned to the UK in 1984. By then she was already pregnant. The immigration officer refused Kumar entry clearance because he believed the marriage had been entered into primarily to obtain admission to the UK, but his decision was overruled by the Court of Appeal. The Court drew attention to the fact that there was evidence of the couple's devotion to one another during their time spent together in India and this should have been taken into account in assessing what must have been the primary reason for the marriage. The leading judge pointed out how easily immigration officers can fall into the trap of treating an admission by an applicant that he wishes to come to the UK as evidence that entry here is the primary purpose behind the marriage. A decision should be reached, he said, on an impression of the evidence as a whole, not upon legalistic analysis. Only if the matrimonial relationship between the couple was of subsidiary importance should entry clearance be refused on the basis of the 'primary purpose' rule. Here it obviously was not.

How have the courts interpreted the requirement that the parties to the marriage, or intended marriage, must have 'met'?

The word 'met' is rather ambiguous, but in the case of *Rewal Raj v Entry Clearance Officer, New Delhi* (1985) the Immigration Appeal Tribunal decided that it meant that the couple must have 'made one another's acquaintance'. In that case the couple had, at least in one sense of the word, 'met' at a ceremony, organised by their respective parents, at which they had been betrothed to one another as children. One of them was four years old, the other only three. Such a 'meeting' did not count for the purposes of the rule, the Court decided. On the other hand, in the case of *Balvinder Singh* (1986) the Immigration Appeal Tribunal ruled that a couple who had met only once, and very briefly at a family wedding when they were twelve and eleven years old respectively, could be described as having made one another's acquaintance. The question is one of fact in each individual case.

If a fiancé or fiancée is granted entry clearance, is he or she under any restrictions?

Yes, he or she will only be admitted initially for a period of 6 months and there is a prohibition on working in the UK during that time. Once the marriage has taken place (usually during the 6 month period) an application can be made to the Home Office for an extension. This will be granted for a period of up to 12 months and the bar on employment lifted. The same rules then apply as are applicable to those admitted as spouses (see below). If the marriage has not taken place within the 6 months, an extension for this purpose may be applied for and this may be granted, provided the Home Office is satisfied that the marriage will take place at an 'early date'.

What restrictions are placed on spouses?

Husbands or wives are admitted initially for a period of 12 months. At the end of this period, the time limit on the stay will usually be removed completely, provided the Secretary of State is satisfied that the marriage has not been terminated and that each of the parties still has the intention of living permanently with the other as his or her spouse. If in doubt, the Secretary of State has a discretion to grant an extension for a further 12 months instead of giving indefinite leave to remain in the UK.

What happens if the marriage breaks down within 12 months?

The Secretary of State has no power under the Immigration Rules to permit an extension of stay in these circumstances, even if the applicant was wholly blameless for the marriage breakdown and it is the other party who was responsible and who no longer has any intention of living permanently with the applicant. However, the Secretary of State may, at his absolute discretion, act outside the Rules and might choose to allow someone to stay if there were compelling reasons of a very special nature. Also if an applicant were to appeal against deportation, compassionate circumstances might be taken into account, including the question of responsibility for the failure of the marriage.

CHAPTER 5

Property matters in nuclear and extended families

In this section we consider some important legal questions relating to the property of the adult members of nuclear and extended families. Evidence from social surveys suggests that while most Asians in Britain now live in separate households comprising a nuclear family unit, a substantial number still follow the traditional pattern of living within an extended or joint family system. Even where members of an extended family do not all live in the same household, there may still be some pooling of financial resources or other co-operative arrangements about the management of money and property.

1 OWNERSHIP OF PROPERTY

Generally speaking, English law does not have any special set of rules to regulate the ownership rights of a married couple or a family. There is, for example, no system in English law of 'community of property' giving joint ownership of family property automatically to both husband and wife or to the extended family. The result is that possessions such as houses, furniture, household appliances, cars and savings in bank and building society accounts basically belong in law to the person in whose name the particular item of property was acquired. The mere fact that a house has been bought as a family home or that the family car is driven by both spouses does not mean that it is jointly owned. If the title deeds of the house and the vehicle registration document are both, for example, in the sole name of the husband then the wife will normally not be regarded as legally a part-owner of either asset. On the other hand, where a house or a bank account is placed in the joint names of a husband and wife, the normal assumption will be that they are joint owners. To this general principle there is an important exception, arising out of the law of trusts. The law here is extremely complicated, but broadly the position is as follows. Usually the person who is not the legal owner will be able to claim a share in the property if he or she has made a substantial contribution towards the costs of acquiring the property and if this sharing was what the parties seem to have intended. So if the family home was purchased for £50,000 in the sole name of the husband and if he contributed £40,000 and his wife contributed £10,000 the house would normally be owned jointly by both of them, with his share being four-fifths and her share one-fifth.

Would the position be the same if the house was bought with a loan from a bank or a building society and his wife helped to pay the monthly instalments on the mortgage?

The principle would be the same, provided the payments she made were regular and substantial but not if they were small and occasional. Her share might also be different depending upon how much she paid in comparison with the amounts paid by her husband.

Would other types of contribution made by the wife entitle her to a share?

There are some cases where a wife has succeeded in claiming a share on the basis of substantial contributions eg through unpaid work in the husband's business, through making improvements to the property by means of hard manual labour, and through paying for household expenses in such a way as to lessen the burden upon the husband of paying the mortgage instalments. However, contributions in the form of looking after the house and the children will not entitle a wife to a share in the ownership of any property. However, if the couple get divorced the position may well be very different — see chapter 8.

Would substantial contributions by a brother, father, son, uncle or other relative of the legal owner be treated in the same way as those of a wife?

Broadly speaking, the answer is 'yes'. A good example is the case of *Singh v Singh* (1985). A house had been purchased in 1966 for £5,300 with the help of a mortgage of £4,200. It had been placed in the name of A, but roughly half of the balance of £1,100 had been contributed by B, his brother. The house had been purchased partly as a home for B and his wife. A's name was the only one on the deeds of the property but the sole reason for this was because he had a

24

larger income than B and was thus able to secure a correspondingly large mortgage. The Court ruled that the house was owned jointly by A and B with each brother being entitled to a half-share.

2 OCCUPATION OF THE FAMILY HOUSE

If the matrimonial home is in the joint names of the husband and wife, both of them are entitled to live there and occupy the property. If the house is in the sole name of the husband and the wife has no share in it on the basis of contributions, she will still have a legal right to live there and she cannot be evicted except through an order of the court. In this latter case her rights are derived from the Matrimonial Homes Act 1983, under which she is also entitled to register her rights of occupation so as to prevent her husband selling the property behind her back without her knowledge or consent. However, this Act (which is substantially similar to an earlier Act of 1967) only applies to a house which has been used at some time as a matrimonial home by the couple in question. In the case of *Syed v Syed* (1980) the parties were a married couple from Pakistan. After their wedding they lived in England with relations and later the wife returned to Pakistan on what was initially intended as a brief visit. However, it was two years before she came back to the UK, by which time her husband had bought a house in his sole name, in which he was cohabiting with another woman. His wife claimed a right to live there, but the Court ruled against her because this particular house had never been used by the married couple as their matrimonial home. This may seem unfair and out of line with people's expectations, but it represents the state of English law at the present time. However, a husband does have a duty to support his wife and provide her with suitable accommodation if she cannot support herself adequately. The point of the case is that she cannot claim a right to live in a particular house owned by her husband, if she has never lived in it with him as their matrimonial home, unless she is a joint owner of the property.

If a man had two or more wives, would each wife be entitled to occupy the matrimonial home?

Yes, the Matrimonial Homes Act 1983 specifically says so. This is subject, of course, to the principle set out above in *Syed's* case about the house having been used as a matrimonial home by the husband and the particular wife who is claiming the right of occupation.

3   VIOLENCE IN THE HOME

Recent reports in the press suggest that 'wife battering' may be as common in Asian families in England today as it is in the majority community. There are now a number of women's refuges in the larger towns and cities, some of them specifically for members of the Asian communities, to which the victims of domestic violence may flee and seek a temporary respite from their ordeal.

What legal steps can a wife take if her husband is violent towards her?

There are a variety of courses of action open to her. One is to claim a divorce — details are given in chapter 6. Another is to report the matter to the police in the hope that they may arrest and prosecute, or at the very least caution, the husband. Often, however, the police are reluctant to intervene in domestic disputes and prosecutions are rarely brought unless the wife has suffered serious injuries. An alternative is to seek an 'injunction' from the court, ordering the husband to stop molesting his wife or even more drastically ordering him to leave the matrimonial home for a fixed period of time (Domestic Violence and Matrimonial Proceedings Act 1976 and Matrimonial Homes Act 1983). The main purpose of the latter type of order is to give the wife a peaceful breathing-space while she decides what to do next, eg seek a divorce, find alternative accommodation herself, return to her family etc. Usually the court will order the husband out of the home for an initial period of three months, but this can be extended if appropriate.

What happens if a husband disobeys an injunction?

He will normally be liable to a fine or else to a short period of imprisonment for contempt of court. In certain circumstances it will not be necessary for the wife to seek further assistance from the court to enforce the injunction; instead a policeman may arrest the husband if he has reasonable cause for suspecting him of having broken the injunction. This means she only has to convince the police that he has molested her or returned to the home after being evicted by court order.

Could a court order one of the husband's relatives out of the matrimonial home if they had acted violently towards the wife?

The courts may well be prepared to do this in certain cases, eg where it would be necessary for the protection of her children or when she has already commenced divorce proceedings against her husband.

4 TRANSMISSION OF TENANCIES

When the tenant of rented accommodation dies, whether the property is a council house or in the private sector, the tenancy is automatically transferred as a matter of law to the deceased's widow or widower, provided she or he was living there at the time of the death (Rent Act 1977, Housing Act 1980). Where the tenant dies without leaving a surviving spouse, certain other members of the tenant's family can succeed to the tenancy provided they have lived in the house with the tenant for a period of at least 24 months (in the case of private rented accommodation) or at least 12 months (in the case of council houses) immediately before the death. Those who qualify as other members of the tenant's family include a parent, grandparent, child, grandchild, brother, sister, aunt, uncle, nephew or niece. Cousins definitely do not qualify to succeed in the case of council accommodation and it is unclear whether they qualify in the case of private tenancies.

5 MAINTENANCE AND SUPPORT

Husbands and wives are under a mutual legal duty to provide reasonable maintenance and support for one another, depending upon who is earning money and who is in need. In practice it is normally the husband who has the obligation to maintain and support the wife, either by purchasing food and clothing etc. for his wife, or by giving her money for housekeeping. Orders for a husband to make regular weekly payments to his wife can be made upon application to the courts if he deserts her or is failing to support her (Matrimonial Causes Act 1973, Domestic Proceedings and Magistrates' Courts Act 1978).

Would a Muslim wife ever be expected to go out to work to support herself?

The tradition has been that Muslim wives do not go out to work to earn their living, but in the modern world it is increasingly common for them to do so, especially if they do not have young children to look after. Much depends upon the values and beliefs of the particular community to which the couple belong and upon the views of the husband's extended family. In the case of *Khan v Khan* (1980) a wife who had been deserted by her husband claimed maintenance from him in the magistrates' court and argued that no account should be taken of her own earning capacity since it was not Muslim practice for a married woman to go out to earn an income. When the case went to appeal, the High Court ruled that it would need to have evidence that this was indeed Muslim practice and that it could not be automatically assumed that this was so. Probably in future cases the wisest course for a wife to adopt if she does not wish her earning capacity to be taken into account, is to provide evidence relating to her own particular family and community to show that it would not be appropriate for her to be expected to go out to work. Sometimes Muslim marriage contracts specifically state whether or not the wife is permitted to go out to work and such a contract would clearly be a material factor for the court to consider. In this particular case, the Court decided that since the parties had only been married for a few months and had no children, and bearing in mind the fact that the wife was only about 19 and was following a course of training, it would be reasonable for the maintenance payments ordered to be made to her to be drastically reduced 12 months after the date of the Court's order. By this time she would be capable of earning a salary.

Can a man be sent to prison for failing to support his wife?

Yes, but it is viewed as a solution of last resort and imprisonment will only be ordered by the court if he has the means to pay and is deliberately disobeying previous orders of the court.

Is a man under a duty to support his parents or brothers and sisters, if they are in need?

No, there is no legal duty placed upon him to maintain or support any adult relative apart from his wife and children (the support of children is dealt with in chapter 9). In practice, of course, it is common for the head of an Asian extended family to support other members such as elderly parents and unmarried, widowed or divorced sisters.

Do the Immigration Rules allow an Asian who is settled here to bring in needy relatives to join him permanently?

The Rules are extremely harsh and restrictive and state that widowed mothers, fathers who are widowers and are 65 or older, and parents travelling together of whom at least one is 65 or older, should only be admitted into the UK for settlement if they have entry clearance certificates and the following conditions are met —

(i)   They must be wholly or mainly dependent upon sons or daughters settled in the UK who have the means to maintain their parents (and any other relatives who would be admissible as dependants of the parents) and adequate accommodation for them, without recourse to public funds.

(ii) They must be without other close relatives in their own country to whom they could turn.

(iii) The above two provisions may be extended to allow entry for settlement to relatives below 65 (other than widowed mothers) but only where they are living alone in the most exceptional compassionate circumstances, including having a standard of living substantially below that of their own country. On this basis admission may be granted to sons, daughters, sisters, brothers, uncles and aunts of whatever age who are mainly dependent upon the relatives settled in the UK.

In the case of *R v Immigration Appeal Tribunal, ex parte Manshoora Begum* (1987) the High Court stated that part of rule (iii) above was so unjust and unreasonable that it was invalid and should be disregarded in future. Manshoora Begum, aged 48, applied for admission to the UK to join her brother who was a British citizen settled here. She was a single woman who lived alone in Pakistan and whose only support came from her brother in the UK, who sent her money and let her have a regular share of the crops produced on his lands in Pakistan. She had been disabled from birth, suffering from partial paralysis. None of her relatives who lived near her had assumed responsibility for her and no one seemed inclined to want to do so. The only reason why she had been refused entry to the UK was because, when account had been taken of her brother's contributions, her standard of living was not 'substantially below that of her own country'. The High Court judge considered this part of the rule totally unjust because it would mean that it favoured those applicants who came from more affluent countries and penalised those from poorer countries. He therefore held that it should be ignored by the Courts and immigration officials. However, exceptional compassionate circumstances must still be proved, as they were in this particular case.

What is the position if the applicant does have close relatives in his or her present country of residence but they are unable or unwilling to help support the applicant?

In the case of *R v Immigration Appeal Tribunal, ex parte Bastiampillai* (1983) the High Court declared that in rule (ii) above 'a close relative to turn to' meant a relative who had the ability to provide some assistance to the applicant, for example by way of a house or else through financial support, so as to make it reasonable to expect the applicant to depend upon that relative rather than upon a child or children in the UK. In *R v Immigration Appeal Tribunal, ex parte Swaran Singh* (1987) the Court of Appeal stated that it was the duty of the immigration authorities to administer the above rules humanely and consider not only whether such close relatives could provide a house or financial support but also whether the parent could turn to them for any sort of need which might afflict an elderly person such as loneliness, isolation, chronic illness, accident or a sudden emergency. Furthermore in the case of *R v Immigration Appeal Tribunal, ex parte Dadhibhai* (1983) the Court ruled that the relative must have not only the ability but also the willingness to provide support, before the applicant is refused admission on this ground.

In what way does the applicant need to be dependent upon a son or daughter in the UK?

To satisfy rule (i) above the applicant may show financial, physical or emotional dependence. If the dependence is financial, it must not have been created deliberately and artificially in circumstances where it was unnecessary. In *Zaman v Entry Clearance Officer, Lahore* (1973) an elderly Pakistani farmer and his wife applied to join one of their sons who was in the UK. They were refused entry because the father was giving away the income from his farms to his other sons who lived in Pakistan. This gift, though it followed customary practice, was considered by the Immigration Appeal Tribunal to be an artificial way of creating a financial dependence on the son in the UK.

6 TAXATION

Hitherto, for purposes of income tax, the income of the husband has normally been added to any income of the wife and the husband has received a 'married man's allowance' (which was higher than a single person's allowance and reflected his duty to support his wife), while the wife received an 'earned income allowance' in respect of her earnings. However, as from the tax year beginning in April 1990, husbands and wives will be taxed independently and their incomes will not be added together. Each spouse will have a separate allowance (equivalent to that of a single person) and there will be an additional 'married couple's allowance' for their benefit.

Can a taxpayer claim an additional allowance if he is supporting an elderly or disabled relative?

No. Such allowances used to be given, but they were abolished from the start of the tax year 1989-90.

7 SOCIAL SECURITY

A wife can obtain certain welfare benefits on the strength of her husband's contributions to the national insurance scheme, even if she herself has not worked or contributed to the scheme. The most important of these so-called 'derived' benefits are a widow's pension and a lower rate (category B) retirement pension.

If a man has two or more wives, can each wife claim these benefits on the basis of the husband's contributions to the scheme?

Here English law takes a very hard line. If a man is validly married to two or more wives simultaneously none of the wives may claim benefits, not even the first wife, despite the fact that the husband has a mandatory obligation to contribute to the national insurance scheme. The rule applies even if only one of the wives is resident in the UK. Many people have argued that the rule is wrong and should be changed.

Is it true that a widow who lives with a man automatically loses her widow's pension?

Yes, this is because of the operation of the so-called 'cohabitation rule'. She will lose her pension for any period during which 'she and a man to whom she is not married are living together as husband and wife'. The state assumes that the man with whom she is cohabiting will support her and therefore she no longer needs the widow's pension. The 'cohabitation rule' also applies in the field of 'income support' (previously known as 'supplementary benefits') so that single people who cohabit cannot each claim income support. They are treated like a married couple and only given one allowance.

How do the authorities define cohabitation?

There are a number of criteria including such factors as whether the couple operate a joint household, the length and stability of their relationship, whether they afford financial support for one another, whether they have a sexual relationship, the existence of any children of their union and whether they try to indicate publicly that they are 'married' by the woman using the man's name. However, although the courts have described these factors as useful guidelines, none of them individually provides conclusive proof of whether the couple are legally cohabiting.

One case where the rule seemed to be very unfairly applied was *Amarjit Kaur v Secretary of State for Social Services* (1981). There a Supplementary Benefits

31

Appeal Tribunal decided that a 28 year old Sikh divorcee and a 72 year old Sikh man were cohabiting as husband and wife. The decision was upheld on appeal to the High Court on the basis of three facts. First, the parties apparently shared the same bedroom, though the Court made it clear that there was no finding that they had ever had sexual relations with each other. Secondly, the woman had done all the washing and cooking in the household. However, it was perfectly natural for her to undertake these tasks, bearing in mind the fact that the man was a friend of her father and she viewed him as an uncle. Thirdly, the couple carefully and deliberately split all the household bills on an equal basis, paying exactly half each, an arrangement which hardly suggests two people are living together 'as husband and wife'. In view of these criticisms as well as the great difference of the parties' ages, and evidence that the Sikh community did not like its single women to live alone, it is thought that the High Court may well have been wrong not to have reversed the Tribunal's decision. The parties did not seem to be cohabiting as if they were a married couple.

CHAPTER 6

Obtaining a divorce in England

The only way in which a couple can be legally divorced in England is by means of a court order (or 'decree') dissolving the marriage. English law may also, however, be prepared to treat a couple as no longer married to one another on the basis of a foreign divorce and this aspect is dealt with separately in chapter7.

1 JURISDICTION

An English court can only grant a decree of divorce if it has the 'jurisdiction' or power to do so. There must be some recognised link between the couple concerned and this country. Two foreigners who merely happen to be here on a month's holiday would not usually qualify. The preconditions are not particularly stringent and merely require that one of the following two tests is satisfied:—

(a) one (or both) of the parties is domiciled in England at the beginning of the divorce proceedings; or

(b) one (or both) of the parties was habitually resident in England throughout the period of one year immediately before the beginning of the divorce proceedings.

In both cases it does not matter whether it is the husband or wife whose domicile or habitual residence here gives the court the necessary jurisdiction, nor does it matter which one of them is actually seeking the divorce. The meaning of 'domicile' is given at pages 3-5 above. A person is 'habitually resident' where he is actually living during the period in question, leaving aside brief visits abroad. Such residence merely entails a regular physical presence in this country with a settled purpose for a particular period of time. There is no need for any intention to remain here permanently or indefinitely, as there is for a domicile of choice.

In *Kapur v Kapur* (1985) the couple were Indian nationals who had married in India. The husband came to England to study law and was given limited leave by the Home Office to stay in the UK for this purpose. While he was in England he sought a divorce in the English courts. The initial question to be decided was whether he had been habitually resident in England for the previous 12 months. The High Court ruled that he had, because he had been residing here with the settled purpose of studying and thus his residence possessed a sufficient degree of continuity to count as 'habitual'. Even a person who is an illegal immigrant could be described as habitually resident in England on that basis.

In the past the English courts did not possess jurisdiction to grant divorces to parties to polygamous marriages, but in 1972 they were granted power to do so by the Matrimonial Proceedings (Polygamous Marriages) Act of that year. The jurisdiction is now conferred by the Matrimonial Causes Act 1973, which replaced the previous Act.

2 THE GROUND FOR DIVORCE

There is only one ground for divorce in England today, namely that the marriage in question has irretrievably broken down. The parties to divorce proceedings are known as the 'petitioner' (the spouse who is claiming a divorce) and the 'respondent' (the other spouse). In order to prove that the marriage has broken down irretrievably the petitioner has to establish one of the five 'facts' listed in the Matrimonial Causes Act 1973 as follows —

(a)   the respondent has committed adultery and the petitioner finds it intolerable to live with the respondent;

(b)   the respondent has behaved in such a way that the petitioner cannot reasonably be expected to live with the respondent;

(c)   the respondent has deserted the petitioner for a continuous period of at least 2 years immediately preceding the presentation of the petition;

(d)   the parties to the marriage have lived apart for a continuous period of at least 2 years immediately preceding the presentation of the petition and the respondent consents to a decree being granted; or

(e)   the parties to the marriage have lived apart for a continuous period of at least 5 years immediately preceding the presentation of the petition.

If the court is satisfied on the evidence as to the existence of any *one* such 'fact' then, unless it is satisfied on all the evidence that the marriage has not broken down irretrievably, it must normally proceed to grant a decree. The first decree issued by the court is called a 'decree *nisi*'; this is converted into a 'decree absolute' by the court at the request of one of the parties, usually six weeks later. It is only after the 'decree absolute' that the parties are legally divorced and thus free to re-marry other persons.

3   INTERPRETATIONS OF 'THE FIVE FACTS'

A number of difficult questions arise in interpreting the meaning of the five facts mentioned above. Some indication of the problems which have or may confront the courts in handling Asian traditions and customs are given below.

(a) Adultery

Can a man commit adultery by having sexual relations with a second or subsequent wife?

If the husband is a polygamist and is validly married to more than one wife in the eyes of English law, then he cannot be committing adultery by having sexual relations with any of his wives. If he was a Muslim domiciled in, say, Pakistan he could lawfully marry up to four wives and all the marriages would be recognised as valid in England (see pages 14-15 above). Adultery involves sexual intercourse by a married person with someone who is not the spouse of that married person. However, if the Muslim husband was domiciled in England rather than Pakistan and he took a second wife in Pakistan, the second marriage would not be valid (see page 15 above). The second woman would not be his lawful wife; he would therefore be committing adultery if he had sexual relations with her and his first (and only true) wife could successfully petition for a divorce if she found it intolerable to live with him.

(b) 'Unreasonable behaviour'

The sorts of behaviour which spouses commonly complain about in petitions based on this fact include physical violence towards them or their children, drunkenness and alcoholism, abusive and insulting remarks, excessive sexual demands and perversions, deliberate neglect and inconsiderate actions, and so on. Sometimes a combination of comparatively minor complaints, which may seem relatively trivial in themselves, can make a spouse's life so unbearable that a divorce is sought. In deciding whether the respondent's behaviour has been such that the petitioner cannot reasonably be expected to live with the respondent, the court has to view the matter from two angles simultaneously. First, it has to assess the question through the eyes of the parties themselves, bearing in mind their characters, personalities and backgrounds as well as the way each has behaved during the marriage. Secondly, the court has to make a value judgement about the standards which the community in general believes ought to be maintained in a marriage. If right-thinking members of society would find certain types of behaviour unacceptable then the court is entitled to declare that a party to a marriage should no longer be asked to put up with them. A variety of Asian traditions raise difficult questions in this context, to which the English courts have not yet had to give answers. Hence the responses given below are somewhat tentative and speculative.

Would a wife be able to obtain a divorce if her husband physically chastised her?

The husband might argue in his defence that his wife ought to be expected to put up with such behaviour if the chastisement was moderate, if it was inflicted as a punishment for wrongdoing or a failure to fulfil a marital obligation and if it was acceptable in the context of the couple's own upbringing, background and culture. However, a husband has no right to beat his wife in English law; indeed such conduct amounts both to the 'tort' (civil wrong) of 'battery' and the crime of assault. If the violence used is at all serious, it seems very likely that the wife would succeed in a petition for divorce.

Can a husband prevent his wife from leaving the matrimonial home or having visitors without his permission?

To impose restrictions of this sort would seem unreasonable to most members of the white majority community, but some Asian communities might find them perfectly acceptable and in keeping with tradition or religious beliefs. In English law the husband is no longer regarded officially as the head of the family, as he is in most Asian communities. He has no formal right to dictate to his wife how she is to behave, whom she can have as her friends, whether she may go out to work or how she is to spend her leisure. Muslim wives, on the other hand, are not expected to mix freely with men, either socially or at work, because they are assigned separate and distinct roles in Muslim society in accordance with religious doctrine. No doubt, an English court faced with a wife's complaint about such restrictions or a husband's complaint that his wife had disobeyed his instructions would do its best to strike a balance between upholding minimum standards applicable to everyone living in England and maintaining the freedom of ethnic minority groups to retain their distinctive cultural practices and identity. The degree of restraint imposed upon the wife would be an important factor and it is hard to believe that a wife would fail to obtain a divorce if she was kept a virtual prisoner in the matrimonial home.

Individual liberty is an important value in English social and political philosophy.

What would be the position if a Muslim couple had a marriage contract which specifically gave the wife the right to visit relatives and friends and to work outside the family home?

This would greatly assist the court in deciding what was reasonable behaviour in the context of the marriage of this particular couple. A husband who tried to prevent his wife from exercising such rights under the contract would clearly be acting unreasonably. On the other hand, if the contract specifically stated that the wife agreed not to work outside the home it might well be held that she was behaving unreasonably if she broke that undertaking, at any rate unless she could provide a reasonable justification, eg her wages were needed to support the children of the family.

Could a 'traditional' husband obtain a divorce on the grounds that his wife's behaviour was too 'modern'?

If, for example, a Muslim wife suddenly began behaving in a 'Western' manner this might gravely offend her husband, both because her conduct was contrary to Islamic principles and because it represented a change from what he had expected when he married her. If, for instance, she stopped wearing a veil, started attending parties and consuming alcoholic drinks or began to break dietary taboos, her husband might feel that he could not continue with such a marriage. Although 'incompatibility' is not itself one of the five 'facts' for divorce, it has been pointed out by one expert that the key question the court has to decide is whether or not it is reasonable to expect the petitioner to live with the respondent, in the light of her altered behaviour. Thus in one case it was decided that a wife could obtain a divorce from a husband who ignored her, led an entirely independent life and refused to tell her what he was doing.

Can a wife obtain a divorce on the basis of 'unreasonable behaviour' if she is ill-treated by members of her husband's family?

In the case of *Devi v Gaddu* (1974) the couple, who were of Indian origin, were living in England with the husband's parents in a single household. The wife complained to the Court that her mother-in-law had behaved badly towards her and in particular had on one occasion attacked her with a kitchen utensil. The Court ruled that in a case like this, where the wife was living as part of her husband's extended family, it was no defence for the husband to say that the wife was suffering at the hands of his mother rather than himself. He knew perfectly well what was going on and instead of shielding his wife from abuse he was standing idly by and allowing it to continue. Although this decision was based on a complaint by the wife to a magistrates' court, the same principles would be applicable in divorce proceedings.

(c) 'Desertion'

For a petition based on the fact of desertion to succeed, not only must the couple have lived apart for a period of 2 years but also the respondent must have intended to desert the petitioner. Intention to desert involves two key elements. First, the separation must not have been by agreement of the couple. The essence of desertion is that it is a wrongful act on the part of the respondent, a matrimonial 'offence'. A consensual separation, by way of contrast, is a mutually agreed arrangement organised voluntarily by both partners. Secondly, there must be no good reason or justification for the respondent to have left the petitioner. A good illustration of this is found in the case of *Quoraishi v Quoraishi* (1985). The couple, who were citizens of Bangladesh and doctors by profession, had married in Pakistan and came to live in England during the 1970s. In the absence of any children of the marriage, the husband asked the wife to accept the idea of his marrying a second wife but she refused to agree to it. Despite her opposition he later contracted a valid second marriage by proxy with a woman in Bangladesh, which was where he was now domiciled. His first wife left him and he then brought his second wife to England. He petitioned the English court for a divorce from his first wife on the basis of her desertion, but the divorce was refused. The judge ruled that the first wife had a good reason for leaving her husband because, in marrying again without her consent, he had taken a grave step which seriously endangered the continuance of the first marriage. The Court took account of the fact that the couple had been parties to a marriage which had actually been monogamous for the previous fifteen years, nine of them spent in the UK, and that the wife had made very plain her repugnancy towards any second marriage by her husband. In reaching this conclusion, the Court was strongly influenced by the decision of the High Court of Allahabad in the Indian case of *Itwari v Asghari* (1960). There it was decided that, in modern conditions, the burden lay upon a Muslim husband who married a second wife against his first wife's wishes, to establish that this did not involve insult or cruelty to his first wife. In the absence of very powerful reasons, such insult or cruelty would be presumed to have been caused. This Indian decision tended, therefore, to show that a first wife who left her husband in these circumstances had a good and just reason for doing so, even if they came from a community in which polygamy was allowed.

If the first wife in Quoraishi's case had herself petitioned for a divorce, would she have succeeded?

Almost certainly. She would have complained that her husband had behaved in such a way that she could not reasonably be expected to continue to live with him, ie she would have used fact (b) above. The court would have borne in mind the background of the parties and the circumstances of their own marriage, including the position under Muslim law, but eventually it would probably have decided, as in *Itwari v Asghari*, that in modern society even a Muslim wife should not generally have to put up with such behaviour unless she specifically agreed to it in advance. This would, of course, be even easier to prove in a case where a marriage contract between two Muslims specifically provided, as not infrequently happens today, that the husband should not marry a second wife without the prior consent of the first wife. In the case of *Poon v Tan* (1974) the English courts decided that a Chinese wife, married according to custom in Singapore, was entitled to a divorce on the basis of her husband's 'unreasonable behaviour' when he attempted to marry a second wife in an English register office.

What is the position if a husband simply orders his wife out of the matrimonial home and tells her never to return?

Desertion does not always have to take the form of leaving one's spouse. Driving a spouse away can also count — it is sometimes referred to as 'constructive' desertion. In appropriate circumstances the spouse who is expelled may alternatively be able to obtain a divorce on the basis of 'unreasonable behaviour'. In *Khan v Khan* (1980) an Indian husband told his wife that if she attended a particular wedding she was never to come back to him again. The wife complained to a magistrates' court, which held the husband to be in desertion. Although this was not a divorce case, the principle would seem equally applicable in divorce proceedings.

(d) Separation for two years, coupled with the consent of the respondent to the divorce

Whereas (a), (b) and (c) above involve a complaint by the petitioner that the respondent has in some way broken a matrimonial obligation and allegations of this nature may obviously entail some hostility and bitterness in the divorce proceedings, fact (d) is available to those spouses who find that they are incompatible but who either cannot or do not wish to make accusations against one another. It is the most 'civilised' way to get divorced, simply requiring mutual agreement upon the obtaining of a decree after the couple have lived apart for a period of at least two years. Usually this will mean that each of the parties must have lived in a separate house (eg the wife having gone back to live with members of her own family or the husband having moved out of the matrimonial home to live elsewhere). However, occasionally it is possible for husband and wife to be regarded legally as living apart even if they are still in the same house, provided they are living in separate 'households'. This might happen if the house was a very large one and the parties not only slept in separate bedrooms but also had no common social or domestic life together. This would mean that they should not eat together and the wife should not perform any of the usual domestic tasks such as washing, cooking, cleaning etc for the husband. It is hardly possible to imagine that an Asian wife, who continued to function in the normal way in a household based around her husband's extended family, could successfully claim she was living apart from her husband if the only aspect of separation she could point to was that she no longer slept with her husband.

(e) 'Separation for five years'

If a couple have lived apart from one another for five years, this provides very strong evidence indeed that their marriage has irretrievably broken down, at any rate where (as the law requires) at least one of the parties has throughout this period regarded the marital relationship between them as dead and finished. If one of them petitions for divorce on this basis the court is extremely likely to grant a decree. However, when this basis for divorce was introduced in 1971, there was concern in Parliament about whether it would operate unfairly against wives who would be cast aside by their husbands even though they had not broken any matrimonial obligations and were wholly innocent of blame for the breakdown. They could now be divorced against their wishes by a husband who had abandoned them for the previous five years. As a result some protection was provided in the form of a defence which a respondent can raise in these five-year separation cases. To succeed in this defence, the respondent has to satisfy the court that a divorce would result in 'grave financial or other hardship' to the respondent and that it would in all the circumstances be 'wrong' to dissolve the marriage. If the court is satisfied that these two elements are proved then it may dismiss the petition and refuse the divorce. In practice the courts tend to reject the defences and grant divorces in these cases. Very occasionally a wife has succeeded in proving that she would suffer grave financial hardship, eg through loss of the chance of obtaining a valuable widow's pension on her husband's death. However, there have been a number of cases in which Hindu wives in India have attempted to prevent a divorce on the ground of grave hardship of a non-financial nature, related to their religious beliefs and social and cultural environment. They have argued that the social and religious attitudes and conventions in their communities in India would result in them

40

being shunned and degraded if they were to be divorced in England. In the case of *Banik v Banik* (1973) the parties had been married in India in 1949. Eight years later they ceased to live together and in 1961 the husband came to England alone. He petitioned for divorce on the basis of five years' separation and was met with a defence by the wife supported by an affidavit (a sworn statement) in which she declared —

> 'My husband knows and knew when he married me that I was a devout believer in the Hindu religion. A Hindu woman looks to the spiritual aspect of dying as a married women rather than for any material benefit. A Hindu woman will be destitute as a divorcee. If I am divorced, I will, by virtue of the society in which we live and the social attitudes and conventions existing in it, become a social outcast ... I and the other members of the community in which we live regard the divorce as anathema on religious and moral as well as social grounds. My husband knows the humiliation and degradation I will suffer spiritually and socially if the court grants a decree.'

The Court of Appeal decided, contrary to the view of the High Court, that this pleading did afford the wife the possibility of establishing a defence because the shame and disgrace alleged, if proved, might show a sufficient degree of hardship. However, when the case was referred back to the High Court for an examination of the evidence in greater detail, it was found that although the wife would have no hope of remarriage, she would not be a social outcast but would merely remain in an unchanged position within her brother's family where she had been since the separation. Her defence therefore failed because, in the Court's view, the hardship was not grave enough: *Banik (No.2)* (1973).

The same result was reached in *Parghi v Parghi* (1973). In this case the parties were well educated sophisticated Hindus, whereas in *Banik's* case they were lower middle-class and the wife was illiterate. In *Parghi's* case the judge decided that the wife's belief that marriage was 'for life' and thus indissoluble, was similar to that of many Christians and stated that she would certainly not be ostracised by the rather westernised community in which she lived in Bombay.

In *Balraj v Balraj* (1981) the wife also failed in her defence. The judge found as a fact that among the 'backward *kshatriya* community' to which the couple belonged, a divorced wife would be in an odd position and certainly at a disadvantage in having no fixed status, since divorce was not recognised in that community. Moreover, the effect of a divorce on the marriage prospects of the couple's daughter would constitute a hardship both for the daughter and for her mother. Despite this, the judge held that, considered objectively, these hard-

41

ships could not be considered grave enough and his ruling was upheld by the Court of Appeal. Even if the hardship had been established to be sufficiently grave, it seems unlikely that in a case like this an English court would have reached the conclusion that it would be 'wrong' to dissolve the marriage. English public policy favours the ending of marriages that have become no more than 'empty shells' and when couples have lived apart for many years in different continents, this is all that is really left of their marriages — at any rate where one of them has long regarded the marriage as over and finished. There is no point in preserving the marital status of the parties in name alone. On the other hand, the English courts are concerned to ensure as fair an outcome as possible for the wife in financial terms (see chapter 8) and in five year separation divorces, they can postpone the grant of the final decree absolute until proper financial arrangements have been made by the husband.

4   PRACTICE AND PROCEDURE

Only about 2% of the 150,000 or so divorce cases brought each year are defended by the respondent and actually argued out in court. Usually the respondent either wants to have the marriage dissolved as much as the petitioner or else he or she comes to realise, within a short time after receiving a copy of the petition, that a divorce is inevitable. The 98% of cases which are 'un-defended' are dealt with by means of a 'special procedure' which is designed to achieve speed, simplicity and economy. The result is that if all goes smoothly a divorce can be obtained in a matter of 7-8 months by filling out some reasonably straightforward forms, and for a cost of up to about £250. If there are disputes over financial and property matters or over children of the marriage these may, of course, take much longer to resolve and be very much more expensive. Legal aid will be available from the state for those of limited means in appropriate cases.

The way the 'special procedure' works is as follows. The petitioner fills out a petition which is in standard form and in which the petitioner indicates the 'fact' upon which the divorce is based (eg adultery, desertion, etc) and explains briefly what evidence will be relied upon (eg for desertion - when the respondent left home and in what circumstances). Both the petition and an affidavit confirming the truth of the statements in it are sent to the county court (from where the forms are obtainable, together with notes for guidance). A copy of the petition is then sent by the court to the respondent to discover whether or not he or she wishes to defend the case. If the case is defended, it will eventually be tried in open court in the normal way, with examination and cross-examination of the parties and their witnesses. If it is undefended, the county court registrar merely checks in his office to see if the petitioner's documents have been correctly completed and, unless he is dissatisfied for some reason, he will pass them on to the judge with a certificate indicating that the case is proved. The judge then formally pronounces a decree of divorce in open court, usually in batches of fifty decrees at a time. Neither party has to be present in court to hear the pronouncement which will subsequently be communicated through the post to both parties.

Is a Muslim wife who obtains a divorce in the English courts truly divorced in the eyes of Muslim law?

This is a controversial question, although the best view is probably that such a divorce is recognised as valid in Muslim law in many cases. However, some Muslim wives feel that they cannot remarry after an English decree unless the husband has also pronounced a *talaq*. He may refuse to do so or else lay down harsh conditions for doing so which really amount to blackmail, such as insisting upon payments of money or the return of dowry or jewellery etc. It is unclear whether the English courts would have the power to order a husband to pronounce a *talaq* in such circumstances since the question has never been put to a judge. An alternative, less direct, method of trying to induce the husband to do so, is to ask the court to penalise him financially if he does not pronounce a *talaq* within a fixed period of time. An order of this nature was made in the case of *Brett v Brett* (1969) in relation to a Jewish marriage (for further details of the financial consequences of divorce, see chapter 8).

CHAPTER 7

Obtaining a divorce overseas

In certain circumstances English law will recognise a divorce obtained outside the UK as valid and effective. The parties will then be free to remarry, either in England or elsewhere, and the English courts will have similar powers to make orders about the distribution of the couple's financial resources and property as on the grant of an English divorce (see chapter 8 for further details).

The rules about the circumstances in which an overseas divorce will be recognised here are complex and are to be found in the Family Law Act 1986. Before examining them in some detail, it may be helpful to explain the broad principles behind them. First, English law appreciates that the *grounds* for divorce differ widely from one country to another and it is not concerned as a condition of recognition to ensure that the reasons justifying a divorce in a foreign country are identical to those in English law. An overseas divorce will not, therefore, be refused recognition simply on this basis. Secondly, however, some *methods* of getting divorced overseas are so different from English procedures that this aspect is thought to be relevant. Whereas English divorces have to be granted through the courts, many systems overseas allow divorces to be obtained without the need to go to court. These types of 'extrajudicial' divorce take various forms including the *talaq* of Muslim law, in which the husband may unilaterally repudiate his wife by oral or written declaration, and divorces arranged by mutual agreement between the spouses, which are lawful under Hindu custom and the laws of several countries in the Far East. English law has rules about recognition which vary according to the degree of formality required for different types of overseas divorces. Thirdly, English law checks to see that the couple have some sort of acceptable connection with the country where they were divorced. For example, an American divorce obtained in Las

Vegas by an Indian couple, resident in England, during the course of a special one-week visit there, would not be recognised. Fourthly, the English courts have been given the discretion to refuse recognition to some foreign divorces simply on the basis that they offend against English ideas of justice and public policy.

1 TWO TYPES OF OVERSEAS DIVORCE

The Family Law Act 1986 divides overseas divorces into two separate categories, each with a different set of rules. The first type are called divorces 'obtained by means of proceedings'. The second type are divorces 'obtained otherwise than by means of proceedings'.

What is meant by the word 'proceedings'?

The Act simply says that proceedings means 'judicial or other proceedings'. Judicial proceedings are easy to understand, namely those occurring through the courts (as happens with English divorces). To comprehend the meaning of 'other proceedings', it is necessary to look at some of the cases decided before 1986.

In *Quazi v Quazi* (1980) a Muslim couple were divorced by *talaq* in Pakistan under the procedure laid down there by the Muslim Family Laws Ordinance 1961. Under the Ordinance, written notice of the *talaq* had immediately to be delivered or sent to the Chairman of the appropriate Union Council and a copy of the notice had to be supplied to the wife. The effect of this notice was to 'freeze' the *talaq* for 90 days, during which time the Chairman of the Council was given an opportunity of trying to achieve a reconciliation between the spouses. It was only after the end of 90 days' delay that the divorce was effective, assuming that no reconciliation had occurred in the meantime. In *Quazi's* case the House of Lords decided that parties who followed this procedure under the Pakistan Ordinance (which is also in force in Bangladesh) did obtain their divorce by means of 'other proceedings', as that expression is understood in English law.

Would a *talaq* on its own count as 'other proceedings'?

In a number of Muslim countries a *talaq* divorce is effective immediately and there is no procedure like that described above in relation to Pakistan. The English courts refer to these simple *talaqs* as 'bare *talaqs*' because they are not accompanied by any notices or delays or the involvement of any administrative councils or authorities. Bare *talaqs* are lawful in such countries as India, Kashmir, Saudi Arabia and the Gulf states.

The case of *Chaudhary v Chaudhary* (1984) shows how English law will regard them. The divorce in question occurred in the Pakistani part of Kashmir which was never subject to the Muslim Family Laws Ordinance 1961 because it is semi-autonomous (self-governing). The English Court of Appeal stated that, from the evidence in the case, apart from the pronouncement of the *talaq* by the husband there was no formality required and no need for any notification of the divorce to anybody (even the wife). No institution of the state, legal or administrative, was involved and no religious institution played any part. Such a simple procedure for getting divorced, the Court ruled, did not amount to 'proceedings' in English law, even though it was laid down by divine authority through the text of the *Quran*. It seems clear therefore that *talaqs* on their own, which merely require a pronouncement by the husband, whether once or three times, do not qualify as 'other proceedings' under the Family Law Act 1986.

So what will the English judges require for 'other proceedings'?

According to the case of *Chaudhary* they will not count merely private acts of the parties themselves, whether performed separately or jointly, even if they are done ceremonially in the presence of witnesses. The judges will require some element of formality derived from the involvement of some agency or institution, whether religious or secular, which is either part of the state machinery or recognised by it. There is no need for this institution or agency to have the power actually to veto the divorce, but its function must be more than merely providing a means of proving the existence of the divorce, ie more than just registering divorces for the purposes of keeping records. This means that systems which allow for extrajudicial divorce by simple agreement of the parties, such as occurs in Hindu, Japanese, Thai and Chinese law, will not be treated as resulting in divorces obtained by 'other proceedings' in English law. Nor will the fact that such a divorce was put into writing and registered with a state official make any difference, unless such registration was a compulsory requirement for the effectiveness of the divorce itself, as it appears may be the case, for example, in respect of *talaq* divorces in Egypt and Iran.

Would a Muslim *khula* divorce qualify as 'proceedings'?

Being merely a consensual divorce, achieved on the initiative of the wife, it seems unlikely to qualify, even if it is put into writing and attested by witnesses. However, if the *khula* was obtained in Pakistan or Bangladesh and notices were served under the Muslim Family Laws Ordinance, it might contain sufficient involvement of an institution (the Union Council) to qualify.

What about the dissolution of Chinese marriages in Hong Kong?

Certain mutually agreed divorces from Chinese marriages in Hong Kong now entail the parties having to give prior written notice in a prescribed form to a designated public official of their intention to dissolve the marriage. The official will interview the parties to make sure that they understand what they are doing and that each of them freely and voluntarily desires to end the marriage. For the divorce to be legally binding, the couple must then sign, in the presence of each other and of two attesting witnesses, a written agreement which will only have legal effect from the time when it is registered. Such compulsory formal arrangements would certainly constitute 'other proceedings'.

Having now categorised all overseas divorces into the two types — those achieved 'by judicial or other proceedings' and those not obtained in this manner — we can next examine the different rules applicable to each category.

2 RULES FOR RECOGNITION OF DIVORCES OBTAINED BY MEANS OF JUDICIAL OR OTHER PROCEEDINGS

Such an overseas divorce will be recognised as valid in England if it is effective in the country in which it was obtained and, at the date of the start of the proceedings, at least one of the spouses was either domiciled there or habitually resident there or else a national of that country. The meanings of 'domicile' and 'habitual residence' are given at pages 3-5 and 33-4. Domicile, habitual residence or nationality are acceptable connecting factors linking the spouses with the place where the divorce was obtained. Only one of the spouses need possess the connecting factor with the country where the divorce was obtained; the other spouse could, for example, be domiciled and habitually resident in England and possess British nationality and the divorce would still be recognised here (but see 4 below).

3 RULES FOR RECOGNITION OF DIVORCES OBTAINED OTHERWISE THAN BY MEANS OF JUDICIAL OR OTHER PROCEEDINGS

These less formal types of divorce are subjected to tougher rules, making it harder for them to be recognised in England. There are three conditions that need to be satisfied if they are to qualify —

(a)   the divorce must be effective under the law of the country in which it was obtained;

(b)   on the date on which it was obtained —

either

each party was domiciled there;

or

one of them was domiciled there and the other party was domiciled in a country under whose law the divorce is recognised as valid;

(c)   neither spouse was habitually resident in the UK throughout the period of one year immediately preceding the date when the divorce was obtained.

The reason for (c) is that if at least one of the parties has been habitually resident in the UK for a year just before the divorce, English law takes the view that any divorce ought to occur here, using formal English judicial proceedings, because these generally offer better safeguards, particularly for wives, than very informal methods of divorce overseas.

4   DISCRETIONARY REFUSAL OF RECOGNITION

Even if the basic requirements for recognition in (2) or (3) above have been fulfilled, the English courts still have a discretion to refuse to accept the validity of an overseas divorce. There are three principal circumstances when they may do this —

(a)   in the case of a divorce obtained by means of proceedings, if it was obtained without taking reasonable steps either to notify the other party of the proceedings or to allow him or her an opportunity to participate in them properly (such an omission could obviously lead to injustice);

(b)   in the case of a divorce obtained otherwise than by means of proceedings, if —

(i)   there is no official document certifying that the divorce is effective under the law of the country where it was obtained;

or

(ii)   where either party to the marriage is domiciled in another country at the date of the divorce, there is no official document certifying that the divorce is recognised as valid under the law of that other country. The idea behind these grounds for refusing recognition is to ensure that there is proper proof of the divorce and its effectiveness. Wherever possible, therefore, the necessary documents should be obtained to facilitate proof of the divorce in England. If they are simply unobtainable, the English courts may be prepared to accept instead in suitable cases expert evidence on the validity of the divorce in the overseas country concerned.

(c)   regardless of whether or not the divorce was obtained by means of proceedings, where recognition 'would be manifestly contrary to public policy'. An example of this would be where a divorce had been obtained overseas by means of fraud or deceit. Another example is provided by the case of *Zaal v Zaal* (1983). An Englishwoman had married a citizen of Dubai in a Muslim ceremony in Dubai. The husband later pronounced a *talaq* divorce in Dubai in the presence of witnesses. He did not, however, formally notify his wife of the *talaq* at the time and only told her of the divorce two days afterwards. The English judge refused to recognise the divorce because it had been done in secrecy from the wife and she had not had sufficient advance warning of it to enable her to enlist the intervention or support of her husband's relatives to try to achieve a reconciliation. In Dubai, as in most other states in the Arabian Gulf, there is no need for notification of the divorce to any official or to the wife for it to be effective — unlike the position in Pakistan and Bangladesh.

5   TRANSNATIONAL DIVORCES

Sometimes divorces may take place partly in one country and partly in another. For instance, a *talaq* divorce might be pronounced in one country and notice of it be sent to another country. Such divorces have become known as 'transnational divorces' and in one case of this type the husband took his appeal as far as the House of Lords. In *Fatima v Secretary of State for the Home Department* (1986) the husband, a national of Pakistan, pronounced a *talaq* in England and sent the required notice under the Pakistan Muslim Family Laws Ordinance to the Chairman of a Union Council in Pakistan, together with a copy to his wife who was living there. The House of Lords agreed with the lower courts that the divorce could not be recognised in England. This meant that the husband was not free to remarry another wife in England and so his attempt to sponsor another woman's entry to Britain as his fiancée failed. Although the decision in *Fatima's* case was given before the Family Law Act 1986, it seems probable that the result in a similar case today would be exactly the same.

What is the legal significance of a Muslim husband pronouncing a *talaq* in England?

So far as English law is concerned, it has no effect upon the status of the couple as husband and wife. As already indicated in chapter 6, the only way a marriage can be lawfully dissolved in England is by means of a decree from the courts. It was partly as a result of this rule that the House of Lords in *Fatima's* case refused to recognise the transnational divorce. They considered that it would be contrary to legal policy to allow a Pakistani husband, resident in England, to divorce his wife merely by posting notices to Pakistan if he could not do so by the pronouncement of a *talaq* here. Otherwise, it would be too easy for him to get round the latter rule. Hence the husband would need to travel to Pakistan and go through all the necessary procedures there under the Muslim Family Laws Ordinance, if he wants his divorce to be recognised in England.

CHAPTER 8

Financial consequences of divorce

The English courts have wide powers to make orders about a couple's money and property following a divorce, whether that divorce was obtained through the English courts or occurred overseas and is recognised as valid in England. The general purpose of such orders is to achieve a result that is as fair as possible to both spouses and also to give priority to meeting the needs of any young children of the family. For convenience we first examine the position after an English divorce and then turn to the situation when the divorce occurred abroad.

1   COURT ORDERS FOLLOWING AN ENGLISH DIVORCE

The courts can make orders that one party (usually the ex-husband) pay the other (usually the ex-wife) regular weekly, monthly or annual payments by way of maintenance and support. They can also order payments of a lump sum of capital as well as transfers of items of property, such as furniture, a car and even the former matrimonial home. Sometimes the former matrimonial home is placed under a settlement or trust so that, for example, it can be used exclusively by the ex-wife and the children up to a certain time (eg when the youngest child reaches the age of 18) and must then be sold and the proceeds of the sale split between the ex-husband and the ex-wife in fixed proportions, such as fifty-fifty or one third-two thirds. On other occasions the former matrimonial home is sold at once or transferred outright to one of the spouses.

How do the courts decide what is a fair order in a particular case?

The Matrimonial Causes Act 1973 requires the court to consider all the circumstances of the particular family and especially a series of factors which are thought to be most relevant. First priority has to be given to the welfare of the children under 18, but many other matters are listed in the Act as follows —

(a)   the income, earning capacity, property and other financial resources which each of the parties has or is likely to have in the foreseeable future, including in the case of earning capacity any increase in that capacity which it would in the opinion of the court be reasonable to expect a party to the marriage to take steps to acquire;

(b)   the financial needs, obligations and responsibilities which each of the parties to the marriage has or is likely to have in the foreseeable future;

(c)   the standard of living enjoyed by the family before the breakdown of the marriage;

(d)   the age of each party and the duration of the marriage;

(e)   any physical or mental disability of either of the parties to the marriage;

(f)   the contributions made by each of the parties to the welfare of the family, including any contribution made by looking after the home or caring for the family;

(g)   the conduct of each of the parties, if that conduct is such that it would in the opinion of the court be inequitable to disregard it; and

(h)   the value to each of the parties to the marriage of any benefit (for example, a pension) which by reason of the divorce that party will lose the chance of acquiring.

There have been numerous cases in which all these matters have been interpreted and analysed by the courts, but no two cases are exactly alike and anyone wishing to know the sort of order the court would make in their own case should consult a solicitor. The law is too complex to be examined in greater detail here.

Is it true that the courts now expect divorced wives to go out to work?

Since the Matrimonial and Family Proceedings Act 1984 there have been provisions in the law designed to encourage ex-wives to become less dependent upon their former husbands and more self-sufficient and also to try to achieve a 'clean break' financially between the parties so that there are no further maintenance payments due. However, a court will only operate these provisions if this would be a just and reasonable thing to do and if it feels the wife can adjust without undue hardship to having her maintenance payments terminated. In the case of a middle-aged (or elderly) Asian wife who has not been in paid employment during the marriage and who has spent her time bringing up the children and looking after the home, it is extremely unlikely that a court would expect her to go out to work or would terminate maintenance for her.

What attitudes do the English courts adopt upon divorce towards dowries and other gifts and payments made between the couple's respective extended families?

The English courts do not have any special rules about such matters. All items of property owned by the husband or the wife or by them both jointly are subject to the powers of the court and any item (including the wife's jewellery and other personal effects) can be ordered to be transferred from one spouse to the other, bearing in mind all the circumstances and the factors listed above (page 54). Since the courts may not be sensitive enough to the particular religious, local or clan customs followed by the two families, it is probably wise to try to come to an agreement (perhaps with the help of a counsellor from the community in question) leading to an out-of-court-settlement. The English courts are increasingly encouraging parties to come to such private arrangements and do not generally interfere unless one side has acted under pressure or in ignorance. Hence the best way of ensuring that traditions about property are respected upon divorce in England is to reach an agreement rather than leave the matter to be decided by the court. The agreement can later be made part of a court order if this is recommended by the parties' legal advisers.

What happens if the parties are Muslims and dower (*mahr*) is payable on divorce?

Under Muslim law there are two main types of dower, 'prompt' and 'deferred'. Prompt dower is payable by the husband to the wife immediately upon the marriage, whereas deferred dower is usually payable on the dissolution of the marriage through divorce or the husband's death. The husband's obligation to pay the dower arises out of the marriage contract and the amount will often be specified in the contract document itself. It sometimes happens that the amount of the dower announced publicly is far in excess of the sum agreed privately. The purpose of inflating the figure for public consumption is to enhance the prestige of the bridegroom's family, but the real amount due from him will be the smaller sum specified in the private contract.

In a suitable case where the amount of dower is fixed and known, the English courts will be prepared to enforce its payment. In *Shahnaz v Rizwan* (1965) the couple had married in India and the contract provided for the dower to become payable upon divorce. After the husband had pronounced a *talaq* in India, the wife successfully claimed £1,400 in the English courts as the sterling equivalent of the sum mentioned in the contract. A similar result occurred in *Qureshi v Qureshi* (1972), a case in which the marriage contract and the wedding itself were both entered into in England. However, it should be remembered that any such payment ordered by the English court will only form part of any decision about the whole of the couple's money and property and all the factors listed on page 54 will be taken into account. The wife might in fact receive the same amount of money or property as part of the overall allocation by the court, whether or not she claimed a specific sum by way of deferred dower. If the amount of the dower is not specified in the marriage contract, the wife is still entitled under Muslim law to receive a reasonable and proper sum calculated by reference to the dower paid for women of similar social status to the wife, notably her close relations. However, the English courts would probably not feel able to assess what the appropriate figure would be in such a case, so no claim seems likely to succeed in these circumstances in this country.

2   COURT ORDERS AFTER AN OVERSEAS DIVORCE

The Matrimonial and Family Proceedings Act 1984 allows the English courts to make financial and property orders after an overseas divorce along very similar lines to those they can make following an English divorce. In deciding what order to make and for how much, the court has to consider all the circumstances of the particular case and take account of all the factors listed above on page 54. However, there are a number of differences between the two procedures and there are more restrictions to be overcome in order to succeed in obtaining an order following a foreign divorce. The principal rules are as follows —

(a) Divorce obtained by means of judicial or other proceedings

The foreign divorce must have been obtained by means of 'judicial or other proceedings', the meaning of which was explained on pages 46-8. The result is that parties to the more informal types of divorce such as a bare *talaq* cannot apply for an order for financial support. This seems rather unfair.

(b) Applicant not remarried

Only those applicants who have not remarried are entitled to apply. Wives who have remarried are assumed to be able to rely for financial support upon their new husbands.

(c) Permission of the court required

A person applying for an order first needs to obtain the permission of the court to do so. Such permission will not be granted unless there are substantial reasons for making the application, ie a reasonably good chance of success. The idea here is to bar, right from the start, applications from undeserving applicants such as ex-wives who have obtained divorces abroad and have already received large sums of money from their ex-husbands under an order of a foreign court. Another example might be a Muslim woman who had already received a very substantial sum from her ex-husband by way of deferred dower.

(d) Jurisdiction of the court

The English courts only have the power to deal with cases where at least one of the spouses has either been domiciled here or been habitually resident in England for at least 12 months at the date of the application for permission, or at the time the divorce took effect abroad, or where the couple have a house in England which used to be their matrimonial home.

(e) Appropriateness of an order

The court has to be convinced that it would be appropriate for an order to be made by an English court, rather than by a foreign court. In deciding this question the following matters are relevant —

   (i)   the connection which the parties have with this country, with the country in which the marriage was dissolved or with any other country;

   (ii)   any financial benefit which the applicant has received or is likely to receive in consequence of the divorce (this would include payments of deferred dower);

   (iii)   where a foreign order for financial payment has been made, the amount of the order and whether it has already been or is likely to be complied with;

   (iv)   whether the applicant had a right to apply for such an order and, if she failed to apply, the reasons for her omission to do so (here it is worth noting that in Muslim law a wife generally has no rights to maintenance for longer than the three-month period of *idda* following the divorce);

(v)   the availability of property in England in respect of which an order might be made and the extent to which any order made here in relation to property abroad is likely to be enforceable there; and

(vi) the length of time which has elapsed since the date of the divorce.

(f) 1984 Act operates retroactively

An application may be made by a person whose divorce took place overseas before the Matrimonial and Family Proceedings Act 1984 came into operation in September 1985. In *Chebaro v Chebaro* (1987) a decree of divorce had been granted in the Lebanon in April 1985 in respect of the marriage of a Lebanese couple who had been habitually resident in England for the previous nine years. The Court decided that it had the power to consider an application made by the wife.

CHAPTER 9

Parents and children

1 THE NATURE OF PARENTAL RESPONSIBILITY

Parental responsibility is a convenient expression to describe the powers that parents (or guardians) have in respect of their children. It is important always to remember, however, that some of these powers may decrease as children get older and closer to 18, the age of 'majority' or adulthood. The powers are also subject to the decisions of the courts and parents may lose their powers if a court decides that these powers are being abused and the welfare of the child requires that parents be deprived of their responsibility. The judges generally operate on the fundamental principle that the welfare of the individual child is the first and paramount (ie overriding) consideration in cases brought before the courts. Furthermore, parents have important duties towards their children and the law is increasingly taking the view that parents are really only given rights so that they can discharge their legal duties to their children properly and efficiently. Obviously one of the most important of these duties is to maintain and support children, and a parent who fails to do so can be ordered by the courts to pay regular sums of money by way of child support.

What sorts of powers do parents have?

The major powers can be listed as follows:

    (i)   the right to physical possession of the child;

    (ii)   the right to decide upon and control the child's educational and religious upbringing;

   (iii) the right to discipline the child, including the right to administer moderate corporal punishment to the child;

(iv)   the right to consent to medical treatment for the child;

(v)   the right to withhold consent to a proposed marriage while the child is between 16 and 18 years of age;

(vi)   the right to administer the child's property and enter into contracts on behalf of the child;

(vii)   the right to act for and represent the child in legal proceedings;

(viii)   the right to choose the child's names; and

(ix)   the right to the child's domestic services, ie help in the home.

It is, however, vital to stress that none of these rights or powers is absolute and parents must not exceed their rights by acting selfishly in disregard of what English law regards as the best interests of the child. Some examples are given here to show the limitations and restrictions imposed by law on parents' rights.

In the case of *R v Rahman* (1985) a Bangladeshi father who was charged with the 'false (ie wrongful) imprisonment' of his daughter (aged 14) argued in his defence that he had only been exercising his right to the physical possession of his own child. Having placed her with private foster-parents in England after his wife had returned to Bangladesh, he later decided he wanted her to return to Bangladesh, the country of her birth. He bought a one-way airline ticket to Dacca for her and a return ticket for himself. He then grabbed hold of her in the street, slapped her face and pulled her hair when she resisted, and then bundled her into a car by force, intending to take her to the airport. She reacted with screams and was rescued by two police officers who happened to be nearby. She later explained that she was about to sit her 'mock' 'O' level examinations and so did not wish to return to Bangladesh at this time. The Court convicted the father of the 'false imprisonment' of his daughter and sentenced him to 12 months in gaol. 'False imprisonment' occurs where a parent unlawfully restrains his child's freedom of movement, ie goes beyond what he is legally entitled to do by way of moderate parental discipline. In similar circumstances a parent might also be guilty of the crime of kidnapping. This offence occurs when a parent takes and carries away by force or fraud his own unmarried child, under the age of 18, without the child's consent or a lawful excuse. In an unreported case in 1987, a Hindu girl was discovered by her family to be having a love affair in England with a Muslim married man. Her father plotted with some friends to snatch her from the women's refuge to which she had fled from her family and then to take her to India for an arranged marriage. The plot was foiled as the men were pushing her into a car. Her grandmother was alerted by her screams and dragged her free. The father and his friends were convicted of a conspiracy to kidnap the girl by the Exeter Crown Court and each was sentenced to three years' imprisonment. A parent who wrongfully takes or sends his child, aged under 16, out of the UK may in certain circumstances also be guilty of an offence under the Child Abduction Act 1984.

To what degree do parents have the right to use corporal punishment on their children?

So far as the correction and discipline of children is concerned, it needs to be stressed that if a parent exceeds the limits of moderation in using corporal punishment, the parent may be charged with a criminal offence (such as assault) and the child may be taken away and placed in the care of the local authority on the grounds that the child is being ill-treated. Whether a particular punishment is moderate and reasonable depends upon the surrounding circumstances such as the age and strength of the child, the wrong which has been committed by the child and the nature of the punishment itself. In the case of *Re H (Minors)* (1987) a North Vietnamese mother and her children had come to England after escaping from North Vietnam. The mother, no doubt damaged emotionally by her own experiences, seemed unable to look after her children properly in this country. The Court found that there were repeated incidents of neglect, ill-treatment and bizarre cruelty by her towards the children. The children became very disturbed and unhappy. Eventually they had to be removed from the mother for their own safety and the Court decided they should be placed with foster parents, with the idea that they should ultimately be adopted. An attempt would be made to find either a Vietnamese or a Chinese foster family so that at least the children's ethnic identity might be maintained. The judge stated that while the solution in a case such as this had to be looked at in the light of the standards of the culture in which the children had been brought up, this could only be relevant insofar as it did not conflict with minimal standards of child care acceptable in England. The mother's treatment of the children had been excessive by Vietnamese standards and grossly excessive by English standards. She had been cruel and lacking in self-control, resulting in severe physical assaults upon the children.

What limits are there upon a parent's right to arrange medical treatment?

While parents generally possess a right to consent to medical treatment on behalf of their children, there is one particular medical operation to which parents cannot lawfully consent, namely the circumcision of their daughters. The Prohibition of Female Circumcision Act 1985 makes it a criminal offence for parents either to perform the operation themselves or to arrange for another person (such as a doctor or midwife) to do it. Female circumcision is practised by Muslims in the Arabian peninsula, Indonesia and Malaysia, but they are not allowed to maintain this tradition here and it will be no defence for them to argue that they are merely performing a religious custom or ritual. Any member of the public who reasonably suspects that parents are planning to take their daughter abroad for such an operation may have the child made a 'ward of court'. This means that the High Court will take over general supervision of the child's life in place of the parents and the child cannot be removed from the country without the Court's permission. Another practice which is considered harmful to children is tattooing and this is prohibited by the Tattooing of Minors Act 1969 in relation to children under 16.

What is the position regarding education?

With respect to the right of parents to control their children's education and religious upbringing, again parental responsibility is by no means unchallengeable and absolute. To take just one example, as we shall see in chapter 11, a Muslim parent who wishes his teenage daughter to attend a single-sex secondary school for religious reasons cannot legally compel the local education authority to provide her with a place at such a school.

2 LEGITIMACY

Who has parental responsibility in respect of a child largely depends upon whether the child is legitimate or illegitimate, so the legal concept of legitimacy needs to be defined. A child is legitimate if either conceived or born at a time when the parents were married to one another. Usually, of course, the baby will be both conceived and born in such circumstances, but one can envisage a situation where, for example, a couple get married after discovering one of them is pregnant by the other; or the husband may die after conception but before the baby is born. In both instances their child is legitimate in English law. In addition, a child of a void marriage is legitimate if, at the time of the act of intercourse resulting in its birth (or at the time of the celebration of the marriage if this was later), both or either of the parties reasonably believed the marriage to be valid, provided the father of the child was domiciled in England at the time of the birth. This rather complex rule can be made clearer by means of an example.

Ali is a Muslim of Pakistani origin who is domiciled in England. He marries Aisha in Pakistan and a year later brings her over to live in England. They subsequently have a child. Many years afterwards they discover that Aisha was only 15 years old at the time of the marriage. The marriage is void in the eyes of English law (see page 14). However, their child will be legitimate because Ali was domiciled here at the time of the child's birth and at the time of conception one or both of the parents reasonably believed the marriage to be

62

entirely valid (either because of ignorance of Aisha's real age or because of ignorance of the English rule banning marriages by parties under 16).

One further situation where a child is legitimate in English law is where the parents marry one another after the birth of their child. The child is then said to have been 'legitimated' by the couple's subsequent marriage.

3 WHO HAS PARENTAL RESPONSIBILITY?

In the case of a legitimate child, both parents are equally entitled to exercise parental responsibility in respect of the child. Moreover, each of them may exercise such responsibility without the need to consult the other, unless the other parent has indicated that he or she objects to what is being proposed. A father can, therefore, on his own enrol a child in an independent school of his choice so long as the mother has not expressed her opposition to this course of action in advance. If she later disapproves of her husband's decision she can try to challenge it in court proceedings.

In the case of an illegitimate child, the mother has sole and exclusive parental responsibility. If the father wishes to exercise any responsibility he must apply to the court.

Parents who legally adopt a child automatically acquire parental responsibility and the child's natural parents lose their responsibility.

In certain special situations parental responsibility may be entrusted to others, eg to a local authority (when a child is taken into care), to a guardian (after a parent's death) or to the court (if the child is made a 'ward of court').

4 PARENTAL RESPONSIBILITY ON DIVORCE OR SEPARATION

When a married couple separate or get divorced, the question arises as to which of them should have parental responsibility over the children and in particular who should have physical care of them. In such situations the physical care and possession of a child is often referred to as 'care and control', whereas wider aspects of parental responsibility such as decisions about education, religious upbringing and medical treatment are usually described as 'custody'. Normally the choice for the English courts is between giving 'custody' to one parent alone, who would then have both physical care and wider parental responsibility exclusively, and giving both parents 'joint custody', so that they continue to share parental responsibility (as during the marriage), while giving one parent (usually the mother) physical care so that she can look after the child's daily needs.

In many Asian societies, where the father is the head of the household the custom may be for children to go with him after divorce, especially as they get older, so that they can be looked after within his extended family. Muslim law, in particular, tends in this direction, with some Islamic 'schools' having fixed ages at which children should be transferred to their fathers. In English law the courts decide all questions relating to custody on the basis that the welfare of the individual child is the first and paramount (ie overriding) consideration, a principle set out in the Guardianship of Minors Act 1971. They are concerned to try to place a child with the parent who can offer the best future in terms of love, care, affection and discipline, as well as provide satisfactorily for his or her material needs. The mother is given physical care and custody in about 80 per cent of cases. The courts are usually reluctant to move a child away from a settled and satisfactory home established with one parent, for fear of disrupting the child's life to an even greater degree than has already been caused by the breakdown of the parents' own marital relationship. Commonly the children remain with their mother at the time when their parents separate and the courts tend to order that they stay where they are already.

What other factors do the courts bear in mind in reaching their decisions?

They consider the conduct of both parents, but only so far as it affects their ability to be good parents, not their failures as spouses. Neglect or ill-treatment are obviously matters that would count against a parent. The courts try, if possible, to keep brothers and sisters together in the same household so that they can give one another support, at any rate where they are quite close in age. They also bear in mind the wishes expressed by the children themselves, but have to take into account that children may be too young to know where their best long-term interests lie and also that they may have been influenced in what they tell the court by one of the parents. However, the older a child is and the more strongly a preference is expressed for one parent or the other, the greater the likelihood that the court will give considerable weight to the child's views. So far as religious upbringing is concerned, the court is concerned to maintain continuity in a child's religious upbringing, as opposed to switching the child from one faith to another, and to protect the child from any harmful social practices which appear to be part of a particular religion (eg the refusal of Jehovah's Witnesses to allow blood transfusions). In a case where the parents are of different faiths, the law does not favour one religion (even Christianity) above another.

What happens in cases of mixed marriages?

In this branch of the law it is not possible to say what would happen in any future case on the basis of past cases because everything depends upon the circumstances of the particular family and the welfare of the individual child involved. However, two illustrations can be given of the courts favouring the solution of joint custody in these types of cases.

In *Jussa v Jussa* (1972) the husband was an Indian Muslim and the wife an English girl. They had married in England and had three children. After the couple separated, the children, whose ages ranged from two to seven, went to live with their mother and a dispute as to their future came before the Court of Appeal. Both parties appeared to the Court to be admirable parents and no criticism could be made of either of them. It was decided that, although physical care and control should be given to the mother because she would be better at looking after the daily needs of such young children, their custody should be shared jointly by both parents. The parents were capable of co-operating sensibly with one another and of reaching joint decisions about their children and it was very much in the children's interests that they should obtain the full benefits of their mixed inheritance, including a knowledge of Islam.

In *Haleem v Haleem* (1975) an Egyptian man had married an English woman here and there were two children of the marriage, boys aged five and one. Following their divorce the parents were given joint custody, while the mother had care and control of the young boys. The father, who was a devout Muslim, was particularly keen that his sons should grow up with a knowledge of Arabic and the Muslim faith, but the Court of Appeal did not feel this was a sufficient reason to justify giving care and control to him rather than to the mother.

Would the courts prefer a 'westernised' parent to one who followed a traditional lifestyle?

There is no reason why they should take such a view. They are only concerned with promoting the welfare of the child. In *Malik v Malik* (1980) the parents were Muslims from Pakistan. The trial judge gave custody (including physical care and control) of the two daughters, aged eight and ten, to their father. He did so because he thought that the mother's traditional lifestyle would lead to the social isolation of the children within the small circle of her family and community. The father, by contrast (a successful businessman), was much more westernised. The Court of Appeal, however, reversed the decision and gave the mother custody on the basis that the cultural patterns of Muslim family life had not been given enough attention by the trial judge and the practical side of the girls' wellbeing should have been accorded more importance. The Court

65

took the view that the father would be able to maintain sufficient contact with the girls through regular visits and meetings.

Is the parent who is not given care and control always allowed regular contact with the children?

Almost always, because the courts believe it is best for children to maintain good contact with both their parents. Occasionally such visits are so disruptive and harmful for a child that they have to be temporarily suspended and in very rare cases they can be stopped altogether. An example of such an exceptional case is *Rashid v Rashid* (1978) where the father had previously taken the children to Pakistan without the consent of the mother (who had been given care and control) during a weekend contact visit. He did not bring them back until the following month. This was in breach of a court order and the children also came back in poor health. Fearing a repetition of such conduct by the father, the mother refused to allow him to visit the children after this and the Court agreed.

Can a parent who is settled in the UK arrange for the entry of a child living overseas, following a divorce or separation?

Under the Immigration Rules an unmarried child under the age of 18 can be admitted for settlement in the UK if one of its parents —

(a)   is settled in the UK and

(b)   has had sole responsibility for the child's upbringing.

It is the second of these two requirements which may prove difficult to establish, although entry clearance officers have instructions not to interpret it too rigidly and literally. In the case of *R v Immigration Appeal Tribunal, ex parte Sajid Mahmood* (1988), for example, a son was refused entry because this second requirement could not be proved. The boy had been born in Pakistan in 1970. The parents were divorced in 1975. The father returned to the UK where he was settled, but the child stayed in Pakistan with his mother and maternal grandparents. After 1981 the child lived with his paternal grandparents. Although the father had provided financial support for the child he had not had 'sole' responsibility for the child's upbringing. This responsibility had clearly been shared with other relatives and so the child was refused entry to the UK for settlement. This does not mean, of course, that the child could not come as a visitor to see his father, eg during a school holiday. Moreover, the Immigration Rules also allow for the settlement of a child with one parent here if there are 'serious and compelling family or other considerations which make exclusion undesirable' — for example, where the other parent is physically or mentally incapable of looking after the child — 'and suitable arrangements have been made for the child's care'. A child under 12 years of age is normally allowed entry under this rule to join the mother, if she can provide adequate accommodation, or to join the father, if there is adequate accommodation and a female relative in the household willing and able to look after the child. Children over 12 usually have to be living in intolerable conditions if they are to gain entry under this latter rule.

5 ADOPTION

Adoption in England can only occur through an order of the court and when such an order is made, it permanently transfers all parental rights and duties from the child's biological parents to its adoptive parents. It thus has very far-reaching effects, not only in relation to questions of parental responsibility but also in other areas. For example, in the law of succession, an adopted child inherits from its adoptive parents rather than its biological parents and a foreign child adopted by a British couple automatically acquires British nationality. In recent years growing concern about satisfying children's needs to have a clear and accurate sense of their cultural identity, has led adoption agencies to try to match children placed for adoption with parents who are of the same or similar ethnic background and religious faith. There is no legal rule stating specifically that this must be done, but it is regarded as good practice for agencies to make special efforts in this regard. They will thus be acting in accordance with the Adoption Act 1976, which also provides that agencies and the courts must have regard to all the circumstances of a case, with first consideration being given to the need to safeguard and promote the welfare of the child throughout his childhood. They are also bound to discover the wishes and feelings of the child, so far as this is practicable, and give them proper weight depending upon the child's age and understanding. Of course, in many cases the child placed for adoption is a baby and this latter requirement is not applicable.

Before an adoption order can be made by the court the child's parents (if the child is legitimate) or the mother (if not) must normally have freely agreed to adoption. There are, however, a number of exceptional cases where the court can dispense with the need for such consent and proceed without it. One obvious ground for doing so is where a parent is insane and therefore cannot give the necessary agreement. Another is where the mother has abandoned her illegitimate child, for example, left her baby on a doorstep or at a railway station. A third and very complex basis upon which a court may dispense with parental agreement is where such agreement is being 'unreasonably withheld'. If a parent has proved unwilling or incapable of caring properly for the child, the court may feel that it is so obviously in the child's best interests to be adopted that a parent

67

who withholds agreement is acting unreasonably. However, sometimes the court will come to the conclusion that the parent is being quite reasonable in refusing to agree to what is a very drastic order, namely the termination of all links with the child. In the case of *Adoption Application No 41 of 1975* an Indian mother had given birth to an illegitimate child which she placed for adoption soon afterwards. She later changed her mind and refused to agree to the proposed adoption going ahead. The question for the Court was whether to dispense with her agreement on the ground that she was withholding it unreasonably. The judge found that the mother genuinely wanted to keep her child and that she sincerely believed that if she was allowed to do so, this would be for the material and physical welfare of the child. Another factor was that the child's proposed adoptive parents were an English couple and the Court accepted that if the adoption were allowed to proceed, the child would always be aware of its differences of birth, race and traditions from the adoptive parents and most of their relatives and friends. The question of the child's sense of cultural identity thus formed an important part of the decision. This case occurred in 1975 and, as we have seen, the modern trend is for agencies to work hard to find adopters of the same or a similar cultural background to the child.

Are adoptions accomplished overseas recognised as valid in England?

Yes, this is normally the legal position, subject to the right of the English courts to refuse recognition if the adoption offends against rules of public policy.

Do UK immigration rules allow children adopted overseas to settle in Britain with their parents if their parents are already settled here?

This is only permitted as a matter of right if there has been a genuine transfer of parental responsibility to the adoptive parents under the law of the foreign country, upon the ground of the biological parents' inability to care for the child and if the adoption was not one of mere 'convenience' arranged simply so as to enable the child to gain admission to the UK. If these two conditions are not satisfied, the only way in which the child can enter is on the basis of the Home Secretary's discretion.

For immigration purposes must the overseas adoption be a formal one?

This question has frequently troubled the English courts, especially where the sponsoring parents are from the Indian subcontinent. Muslim law does not allow for formal adoptions (partly because of the disruptive effect this might have upon rights of inheritance), but less formal arrangements amounting to a permanent transfer of parental responsibility to the adoptive parents seem to be authorised under tradition and custom in parts of the subcontinent and Muslim law itself permits the informal adoption of orphans and foundlings. The difficulty for immigration officers is to distinguish between those cases where these types of arrangement involve true adoption and those where they really only amount to the temporary care and fostering of children. In the case of *Immigration Appeal Tribunal v Tohur Ali* (1988) the applicant child Tohur, who was from Bangladesh, had been denied entry to the UK to join his sponsor, who claimed to be his adoptive father. His sponsor had originally taken Tohur into his household in Bangladesh upon the death of Tohur's own father, who had sought assurances as he was dying that his relations would provide Tohur with a home. The immigration adjudicator decided that since there was no legal recognition of adoption in Bangladesh, Tohur could not be described as the adopted child of his sponsor; a legally recognised adoption process was required. On appeal to the High Court, however, the decision was reversed. The judge ruled that the key question was whether the relationship established between the sponsor and the child was a permanent one. If it was, this could amount to adoption for the purposes of the Immigration Rules. This ruling was upheld by the Court of Appeal.

Where no adoption has occurred abroad the Home Secretary may, in the use of his discretion, allow the entry of a child into the UK for the purpose of being adopted here under English law, provided the intention to adopt is genuine and not a device to gain entry (details of exactly how the process works is given in a Home Office letter known as "RON 117"). However, apart from this discretionary procedure, there is no system whereby children can be brought into Britain with a view to their adoption here. Once they are here, however, an application to adopt can be considered by the courts and, in deciding whether or not an adoption order should be made, the first consideration is the need to safeguard and promote the welfare of the child up to the age of 18. If there are signs that the real purpose of the adoption is to secure the child's residence status in the UK and especially if the child is already approaching the age of 18, the court may refuse to make the order. The Home Office should be notified in advance of any adoption application planned in respect of a foreign child by a British citizen.

CHAPTER 10

Questions of inheritance

It appears to be quite a common practice in England for members of a deceased person's family to make informal arrangements among themselves for the distribution of the estate, regardless of what the law says about inheritance rights. There is no objection to this if everyone agrees. What follows in this chapter, however, is a description of the strict legal position, which will apply if formal steps are taken to settle the administration of the estate or if a dispute is taken before an English court.

Under English law the inheritance of 'immovable' property, ie land and buildings, is governed by the law of the place where the property is located. So if a man has one house in England and another in India, the inheritance of each house will be decided in accordance with the law of the respective country where the property is situated.

On the other hand, so far as all other items of property (ie movables) are concerned, the law regulating their inheritance is the law of the deceased's domicile at the time of his death. The meaning of domicile is given on pages 3-5. Since many Asians are now domiciled in England, this means that the inheritance even of movable items of property located in, for example, the Indian subcontinent is governed by English law. Equally, in the case of the many Asians who still retain their domiciles of origin in countries in Asia, the inheritance of furniture, cars, household appliances etc. located in England is controlled by the law of the country of domicile, and not by English law. If a case comes before the English courts, they decide it according to whatever law is appropriate in terms of the above rules.

English law divides inheritance into two categories, namely 'testate' succession (where the deceased has made a valid will) and 'intestate' succession (where no valid will has been made).

1 TESTATE SUCCESSION

Any adult person of sound mind can make a valid will by complying with the necessary formalities. These usually concern such matters as whether the will needs to be in writing and signed and whether witnesses need to be present. English law recognises a will as valid if it was correctly and properly made (or 'executed' as lawyers put it) according to the law of any one of the following countries —

(i)   where it was actually made; or

(ii)   where the deceased was domiciled when he made the will or when he died; or

(iii)   where the deceased was habitually resident when he made the will or when he died; or

(iv)   where he was a citizen when he made the will or when he died.

With such a variety of possible legal systems under which a will can be recognised as validly executed, the chances are high that a will made either in England or overseas will be recognised and given effect to in English law.

With regard to the distribution of the property forming the estate of the deceased, English law (unlike Muslim law, for example) does not insist that any fixed part or portion must be allocated to specified relations of the deceased. A person who makes a will is basically entitled to choose freely to whom his property should pass by way of inheritance, subject only to claims for 'family provision' (discussed below).

Does this mean that a man could leave all his property by will to a friend or to his mistress and neglect the needs of his family?

Yes, there is nothing unlawful in him doing this. However, members of his family may be able to make claims upon his estate by means of application to the English courts (see further on pages 75-7, for 'family provision' claims).

2 INTESTATE SUCCESSION

The majority of people die intestate, ie without having made a will, and the following rules apply to the distribution of their estates. The rules are meant to reflect what a reasonable person would have wanted to happen to his or her property on death.

Three situations need to be examined —

(a) Where the deceased leaves a surviving spouse and issue

(i) The surviving spouse receives the 'personal chattels' absolutely: these include household and personal items such as furniture, cars, jewellery, books etc., but not articles used for business purposes; nor money, shares and other investments (which constitute part of the 'residue').

(ii) The surviving spouse receives a 'statutory legacy' of the first £75,000 out of the residue, ie out of the rest of the estate apart from the 'personal chattels'. This means that if the total value of the residue is £75,000 or less, the surviving spouse will receive all of it.

(iii) If the residue exceeds £75,000, the surviving spouse receives in addition to the statutory legacy a life interest in half the excess (a 'life interest' means the income from the property for the rest of that person's life, but without the right to transfer the capital sum). The balance, subject to this life interest, goes to the deceased's issue. The deceased's issue are his children (including legitimated, adopted and illegitimate children) and they are entitled in equal shares. If any child dies before the deceased but leaving his or her own children, these children would take their parent's share (dividing this share equally if there were more than one of them).

(b) Where the deceased leaves a surviving spouse but no issue

(i) If the deceased left not only a surviving spouse but also a parent or a brother or sister (or their issue), the surviving spouse receives the personal chattels absolutely, plus a statutory legacy of the first £125,000, plus a half of any balance absolutely. The other half of the balance over £125,000 goes to the parent(s) if any, or if none are alive, to the brother(s) and sister(s) (or if they died before the deceased, their issue).

(ii) If the deceased left no such close relatives and only a surviving spouse, then the surviving spouse receives the whole estate absolutely.

73

(c) **Where the deceased leaves no surviving spouse**

(i)   If he or she left issue, the whole estate is shared between them; the children take in equal shares and any who die before the deceased leaving their own children are replaced by these children as in (a)(iii) above.

(ii)   If there is no issue, the whole estate goes to the deceased's parents.

(iii)   If there are neither issue nor parents, the estate goes to the deceased's brothers and sisters (or their own issue if they are no longer alive).

(iv)   If there are none of these, then the estate goes to the grandparents.

(v)   In the absence of any grandparents the estate passes to the deceased's uncles and aunts (or their issue if they are no longer alive).

(vi)   If there are no cousins to receive the inheritance, the deceased's estate passes to the British Crown.

In the above rules a 'surviving spouse' does not include a former spouse who has been divorced from the deceased, nor a spouse who was living separately and apart from the deceased at the date of death under a decree of 'judicial separation'. Nor is a person whose marriage to the deceased was invalid in the eyes of English law (see pages 9-10,13-15) regarded as a 'surviving spouse'.

What should an Asian do if he wishes his property to be inherited according to a system other than the English intestacy rules?

He should make a valid will specifying in detail exactly how his estate should be distributed. He is entirely free to do this, subject to the risk of 'family provision' claims (see pages 75-7). Of course, a will may easily become out of date as relatives die and children are born, so a will may constantly need to be revised and updated. This can be achieved by means of additions and amendments, or by making an entirely new will to replace the old one.

Can a Muslim validly make a will declaring that he wishes his estate to be distributed according to Islamic law?

If such a will specifies which 'school' of Islamic law is to govern the distribution, so that the deceased's intentions are clear and unambiguous, then the will should basically be recognised as valid by English law. Approval has been given to such forms of will by Muslim leaders in England and it appears that the directions given in these wills have been duly carried out by the executors. There is, however, one very remote risk in making such wills, namely that an English court might, if the inheritance was contested in legal proceedings, refuse to give effect to those provisions of the Muslim law of succession which might be regarded as offending against principles of English public policy. One example of such a provision is the Muslim rule that in certain circumstances the share allocated to a female heir is only half that allocated to a male heir. Another is that non-Muslims are automatically barred from succession to the estates of Muslims. On grounds of public policy, English law is sometimes unwilling to recognise and enforce rules of a foreign legal system which are felt to be discriminatory and the Muslim rules just mentioned do clearly discriminate on the grounds of sex and religion respectively. If an English court did consider that such distinctions would operate in a fundamentally unfair way in a particular case involving, for example, claims to inheritance by a Muslim daughter or by a son who had converted to a different faith, the discriminatory provisions of Islamic law would be disregarded. It is important to emphasise, however, that there has not yet been a case in which this question has been tested in the English courts and the likelihood is that the terms of the will would be upheld as valid, and full effect would be given to the deceased's wish to have his estate distributed strictly in accordance with Islamic principles. Another method by which the terms of such a will might be challenged and overridden is through a 'family provision' claim, and attention is next turned to such claims.

3 FAMILY PROVISION

This is a system whereby certain relatives and dependants of the deceased can be awarded 'reasonable provision' by the courts out of the estate on the basis that they have been treated less than fairly and adequately, either through the deceased's will or through the rules of intestate succession. It is vital to appreciate, however, that there is a fundamental difference in concept between wills and intestacy, on the one hand, and family provision on the other. A beneficiary under a will or the intestacy rules has an automatic entitlement without any need to go to court. An applicant for family provision has no such rights and must apply to the court for the exercise of discretion in his or her favour. Clearly the rights of beneficiaries under a will or on an intestacy are not absolute since they may be reduced by the court's family provision order, but they remain far stronger than the mere power to apply for family provision.

Family provision claims can only be made against the estate of a person who was domiciled in England at the time of his or her death.

The following persons are entitled to apply for a court order in their favour under the Inheritance (Provision for Family and Dependants) Act 1975 —

(i)   a surviving spouse who has not remarried (including all the wives of a deceased polygamous husband; in the case of *Re Sehota* (1978) the first wife was allowed to make a claim after the husband had bequeathed all his property to his second wife);

(ii) a divorced spouse who has not remarried;

(iii) any child of the deceased (including an adopted child) and any child whom the deceased treated as a child of his family during any marriage to which he was a party;

(iv) any other person who immediately before the deceased died was being maintained either wholly or partly by the deceased, in the sense that the deceased was making a substantial contribution towards his or her reasonable financial needs (this could obviously include a wide range of persons within the deceased's extended family).

The ground upon which the application has to be made is that the distribution of the deceased's estate, either through his will or through the operation of the intestacy laws, is not such as to make reasonable financial provision for the applicant. A widow who has been omitted from her deceased husband's will is likely to be awarded a much larger share of his estate than any other applicant and adults who are wage-earners or who are otherwise comparatively well-off may find their claims being rejected by the courts, in the absence of special circumstances.

The question of whether or not a will makes reasonable provision for an applicant has to be judged on the basis of the parties' legal rights under it and not on the basis of any informal family agreement that individuals will not enforce their legal rights. A formal agreement to compromise and settle an inheritance dispute will usually be binding, but informal assurances will not prevent the court ruling on the question of family provision. In the case of *Rajabally v Rajabally* (1987) the deceased was survived by his widow and their two sons, together with a son of his by an earlier marriage. Under the terms of the deceased's will his estate was left to these four survivors in equal shares, but the only asset was the former matrimonial home which had a value of about £50,000. The widow did not want the house to be sold because obviously she would not be able to find satisfactory and equivalent accommodation with only her quarter-share of the proceeds of sale. She therefore made a claim to the whole house under the 1975 Act. Meanwhile her sons gave assurances to the court that they would not insist on their rights under the will and the son by the deceased's first marriage agreed to have his quarter-share bought out by the widow with the help of a loan. Although the trial judge was satisfied with this solution, the Court of Appeal decided that he had adopted the wrong approach. These informal assurances had to be ignored in determining whether the *will* had made reasonable provision for the widow. Clearly it had not given her a fair share of the estate, bearing in mind the fact that she had been married to the

76

deceased for over 20 years and had gone out to work to help pay off the mortgage instalments on the house. The Act specifically states that in the case of a widow (or widower) the court must bear in mind the age of the applicant, the length of the marriage and the contribution made by the applicant to the welfare of the family, including any contribution made by looking after the home and caring for the family. Here the widow needed to have a secure future in the house so the Court ordered that the property should be transferred into her sole name, subject to a new mortgage being taken out to pay the son of the deceased's first marriage a legacy of £7,500.

One possible criticism of this decision is that it did not give sufficient weight to the respective needs of the parties, an important factor which is expressly mentioned in the Act. The widow's need was principally to continue to occupy the house indefinitely rather than necessarily to own it. On the other hand, the son who obtained the legacy of £7,500 received much less than the £12,500 he was due to obtain under the will and yet he had great needs because he was mentally ill and had very limited prospects of working and earning a living. The mental or physical disability of any of the parties is also a factor the courts have to bear in mind in reaching their decisions.

CHAPTER 11

Children at school

1 THE ORGANISATION OF SCHOOLING

There are three main types of school in England today — county schools, voluntary aided schools and independent schools. The first group, 'county' schools, are more commonly known as 'LEA' schools because they are owned, financed and staffed by LEAs (local education authorities). The large majority of children attend such schools. The second category, voluntary aided schools are owned by voluntary bodies (such as religious organisations), but they are given very substantial aid by the local education authority. The voluntary body appoints the majority of the governors of the school and the governors control the admission of pupils and appoint the teachers. However, the LEA is responsible for the maintenance and repair of the interior of the school buildings as well as for all other educational expenditure, such as the salaries of the teachers. The governors are obliged to pay for the upkeep and maintenance of the exterior of the buildings and for making any improvements, but they are entitled to a government grant to cover such capital expenditure of up to 85 per cent of the cost. The third type of school, namely independent schools, are wholly owned, financed and run by private organisations. Most of these are religious or charitable foundations, but some are primarily concerned with commercial considerations, ie with running the school as a profitable business. They are sometimes referred to a 'public' schools which is very misleading since they are not in public ownership. Independent schools do in fact form the private sector of education, while LEA and voluntary aided schools are part of the state (or 'maintained') sector. There are only about 2,300 independent schools compared with around 4,300 voluntary aided schools and about 16,000 LEA schools.

Who pays the fees at these different types of school?

The local education authority is responsible for the fees in respect of pupils at LEA and voluntary aided schools, whereas parents or guardians are obliged to pay the fees of pupils at independent schools. There are, however, a few 'assisted places' at some independent schools which involve the Department of Education and Science (DES) paying all or part of the tuition fees of pupils who come from families who cannot afford to pay the full fees themselves. These places are allocated upon academic merit through a process of selection.

How does a parent select a suitable school in the state sector?

By law, information has to be published by LEAs and the governors of voluntary aided schools so as to assist parents in making an appropriate choice of school. This information has to cover a number of matters about which Asian parents may be particularly concerned, eg whether the school is co-educational or single-sex, whether it is linked to any religious denomination or group, particulars relating to religious instruction and sex education, the school's policy or rules about dress and uniform, and the public examinations for which pupils will commonly be entered.

Once a parent has chosen a particular school for a child, does the child have a legal right to go to this school?

No, the school is not automatically bound to admit the child as a pupil. The parent only has a legal right to express a preference. Under the Education Act 1980 the LEA has a duty to comply with the preferences expressed by parents provided —

(i) compliance would not prejudice or interfere with the provision of efficient education or the efficient use of resources; and

(ii) if the preferred school is a voluntary aided school, compliance would be compatible and consistent with any arrangements between the governors and the LEA in respect of the admission of pupils; and

(iii) if the preferred school is academically selective, compliance would be compatible with the operation of the selection process.

Some illustrations may help to make the position clearer.

● Mr and Mrs Hassan express a preference to the LEA that their daughter should attend the only secondary school solely for girls within their area. The school is already completely full. The LEA may refuse to comply with the parents' preference under (i) above because to do so would interfere with efficient education at this school by admitting more pupils than the school can physically cope with.

80

- Mr and Mrs Singh have expressed a preference for their son to go to a voluntary aided school which is run by a Roman Catholic foundation. The LEA and the foundation have agreed that normally only the children of Catholics will be admitted as pupils. The LEA may justify its refusal to comply with Mr and Mrs Singh's wishes by reference to (ii) above.

- Mr and Mrs Lim have indicated a preference for their child to go to a particular grammar school. Admission to the school is on academic merit by passing an entry examination, but the Lim's child has failed the examination. The LEA can refuse admission under (iii) above.

Can dissatisfied parents appeal against LEA decisions?

Yes, the Education Act 1980 allows parents to appeal against allocations of children to particular schools. Such appeals are heard by special committees whose decisions are binding on the LEA. Parents are given the opportunity to address the committee in person and they may be accompanied by a friend or appoint someone else to argue the case on their behalf.

Is it lawful for a Muslim father to keep his daughter away from a co-educational secondary school for religious reasons?

Many strict Muslims believe adolescent girls should be separately educated from boys as part of the doctrine of *purdah* (seclusion), but if no places at single-sex schools are available, parents still have a duty to send their children to school. If they fail to do so after a 'school attendance order' has been served on them by the LEA, they risk both prosecution and having the child removed from their care by a juvenile court and placed in the care of the local authority social services department. In *Bradford Corporation v Patel* (1974) a Muslim father had refused to comply with a school attendance order in terms of which his fifteen year old daughter had been allocated to a co-educational school in Bradford. He had been keeping her at home for the previous two years because of his religious objections to co-educational schools and these were the only type of school available in his area. He was charged with an offence under the Education Act 1944 and convicted despite his religious beliefs. Children can only be educated at home if the LEA is satisfied that very high standards of tuition are being strictly maintained and the only other alternative (for those parents who can afford the fees) is to send their daughter to an independent school. There are about 500 independent schools for girls in the UK.

Can any person or organisation establish an independent school?

Yes, any individual or group can set up a private school and charge fees for tuition. However, such schools must, by law, be properly registered with the Department of Education and Science (DES). Failure to do so amounts to a criminal offence under the Education Act 1944. Even so, the system for obtaining registration is reasonably flexible. An application for registration has to be made within one month of the first operation of the school and registration can be granted provisionally while checks are carried out by HM Inspectorate of Education. The main purpose of these checks is to satisfy the Secretary of State that the school premises are suitable, that the accommodation is adequate, that the teachers are competent and that the instruction provided is suitable and efficient. The Inspectors may well criticise a school if the curriculum is too narrow, if the teaching fails to stimulate the pupils to think independently and discuss the material presented, if insufficient time is devoted to secular education as opposed to religious instruction, if the teachers do not possess the normal professional qualifications and if the buildings are in a poor state of repair and do not provide satisfactory surroundings for the pupils. If the criticisms are severe, they may well lead the Secretary of State to issue a complaint to the school under the Education Act and ultimately this may result in the compulsory closure of the school if the matters criticised are not corrected. There has recently been a tendency for reports by the Inspectorate to be quite critical of separate religious schools set up by certain Jewish Orthodox, Christian fundamentalist and Muslim organisations, but in the case of *R v Secretary of State for Education and Science, ex parte Talmud Torah Machzikei Hadass School Trust* (1985) the High Court ruled that, in assessing the quality of education provided by an independent school, such education would be 'suitable' under the Education Act if it primarily equipped a child for life within the particular religious or ethnic community of which it was a member, rather than life within the community as a whole, so long as it did not close off the child's opportunity to choose another form of lifestyle in later years. The Court stressed the need for the Secretary of State to be sensitive to the traditions of minority sects and to take full account of the wishes and religious convictions of the parents of pupils at the school, while still rightly trying to maintain a minimum standard for all schools.

The financial benefits of voluntary aided status are clearly very attractive. How easy is it for a private school to convert to this status?

The majority of denominational schools, ie those run by religious organisations, are now voluntary aided within the 'maintained' sector of education and thus receive large subsidies from the state through the local education authorities. Most are run by the Church of England or by Roman Catholic foundations, but there are also a few Jewish schools of this nature.

Many parents favour such schools not only because their own beliefs and values are shared by the teachers but also because the schools are generally run on disciplined lines and possess an atmosphere which encourages the full development of their pupils.

In recent years considerable interest has been expressed by a small number of Asian groups in the establishment of such schools for Muslims, Sikhs and Hindus. They see particular advantages in the creation of such schools for the proper teaching of religion and instruction in the mother-tongues of the pupils. So far no such school has been given voluntary aided status despite some vigorous campaigns, such as that organised by the trustees of the Islamia Primary School in the London Borough of Brent. One practical problem is that, with the decline in the number of births during the 1970s, the number of school places needed has decreased markedly and thus there are already surplus places at existing maintained schools. With falling school rolls, the DES is not at all keen to extend voluntary aided status to more schools than have it at present because of the large costs involved. The approval of the DES has, by law, to be obtained first and the Secretary of State has rejected a number of applications during the past few years. There were about 400 fewer voluntary aided schools in 1987 than there were in 1981.

Despite this there can be no objection in legal principle to the establishment of voluntary aided schools for Muslims, Hindus or Sikhs. Although some people oppose the idea because they feel it would be divisive, the same argument could be made about Jewish or Roman Catholic schools and in any event there are already about 60 LEA schools where the proportion of pupils from ethnic minority backgrounds exceeds 90 per cent. However, it is still probably true to say that a large majority of Asian parents would prefer their children to go to schools in which there are children from a variety of religious and cultural backgrounds so that they can be integrated more easily into the wider community. Segregation of children along religious lines, if implemented on a large scale, could breed resentment and misunderstanding between different communities, with the possible risk of major confrontations in the inner cities.

How will the new process of 'opting out' work?

Under the provisions of the Education Reform Act 1988, it will be possible for individual schools currently run by local authorities to choose to be released from the control of the LEA and instead obtain their funding direct from central government. They will thus become 'direct grant' schools maintained by the Department of Education. In order to achieve this the school governors will normally need to obtain a majority of votes in favour cast by parents in a secret postal ballot, as well as the approval of the Secretary of State for Education.

What is the new 'open enrolment' policy?

When the Education Reform Act 1988 comes fully into force, every LEA school will be required to admit pupils to the limit of its physical capacity. At present LEAs regulate the numbers of pupils at the various schools in their areas in order to plan ahead and achieve the right balance of pupils and they try to keep small schools in operation at a time of falling rolls. Under the 1988 Act there is a risk that if one local school becomes far more popular than others, it will have to take more pupils than at present with the result that the other schools in the area are forced to close down through lack of enough pupils to be financially viable. The dispute at Dewsbury during 1987-88 was partly concerned with this sort of issue. A number of white parents had expressed a preference for their children to attend Overthorpe School, but Kirklees LEA allocated them instead to Headfield School in which 80 per cent of the pupils were of Asian origin. The parents complained to the Secretary of State for Education that Overthorpe was not full to its physical capacity, but the Minister refused to interfere with the decision of the LEA because, in his view, it had acted within the law as it then stood and it had made a reasonable allocation of pupils to the two schools. Unfortunately, the LEA eventually had to change its decision because it had supplied erroneous information to the parents, and the 1988 Act may further encourage white parents to attempt to move their children away from excellent multiracial schools such as Headfield for no good educational reason at all. However, there is no reason why Asian parents should not apply to the same schools as those specially favoured by white parents if they wish to do so. In this way the segregation of children by colour or culture may be avoided.

2 RELIGIOUS EDUCATION

(a) Collective worship

The Education Reform Act 1988 states that all pupils at LEA and voluntary aided schools (including sixth formers) must, on each school day, take part in an act of collective worship. The arrangements for this collective worship may provide for a single act of worship for all pupils or for separate acts of worship for pupils in different age groups or in different classes or other school groups. However, parents who do not wish their child to attend such worship are legally entitled to insist that the child be excused from attendance. They need merely request the child's withdrawal from such worship. In LEA schools the act of worship is not allowed to be distinctive of any particular 'Christian denomination', but it is required to be 'wholly or mainly of a broadly Christian character'. This does not mean that every single day's worship has to be Christian in character. It is sufficient if, taking the school term as a whole, most acts of worship are wholly or mainly of a broadly Christian character. Before the 1988 Act, in many LEA schools with substantial numbers of non-Christian pupils, the tendency was to include within morning assemblies materials from a variety of faiths and there is no reason why this pattern should not continue under these new provisions. The 1988 Act specifically states that, in working out the form of collective worship to be adopted, individual schools may themselves decide what is appropriate and in the process have due regard to the family backgrounds of their pupils. Moreover, in certain circumstances a LEA school may be exempted from the requirement that acts of collective worship be wholly or mainly of a broadly Christian character if the LEA's 'Standing Advisory Council on Religious Education' (SACRE) decides that this would not be appropriate. In such circumstances the worship could be distinctive of a non-Christian faith, either in the case of the school as a whole or in relation to any class or group of pupils (eg those who are non-Christian). Alternatively, a SACRE may specify in its exemption 'acts of worship which give no emphasis to any one particular religion', as the Ealing SACRE did in June 1989 in relation to four schools in Southall which were the first to gain exemptions under the Act. In the light of all this, there may often be no reason why Asian parents should feel the need to withdraw a child from attendance at worship in a LEA school. On the other hand, in voluntary aided schools the act of collective worship can usually be expected to conform, quite legitimately, with the particular religious denomination of the school concerned and there may thus be a stronger justification for withdrawal in the case of a child who is not of that faith.

(b) Religious education classes

So far as religious education in class is concerned, the 1988 Act specifies that religious education is a compulsory part of the basic curriculum for all pupils (including sixth formers), while also permitting parents to withdraw their children from such classes by requesting that they be excused from attendance. Furthermore if parents wish their child to receive a form of religious education which is not provided at the school they can demand that the LEA make suitable arrangements for the child to receive it at another maintained school or, if that is not convenient, elsewhere during school hours (at the beginning or end of the school day or session). In certain limited circumstances such separate tuition can take place at the child's own school, as we shall see.

Whether or not an Asian parent is satisfied with the religious education offered at the child's own school may partly depend upon the type of school attended. At LEA schools the religious education has to be provided in accordance with what is known as the 'agreed syllabus' and must not be given in the form of doctrines which are distinctive of any particular denomination. The syllabus is agreed at a conference of four committees appointed to represent the LEA, the teachers' associations, the Church of England and such Christian and other denominations as reflect the principal religious traditions of the area. The original 'agreed syllabus' of each LEA was drawn up soon after 1944 and concentrated mainly on biblical studies, but in most counties (and especially in those areas where there are significant numbers of non-Christian pupils) these syllabuses have been revised and updated in recent times to include all the main world religions. Even in areas where such reforms have not been undertaken, the teachers have been able informally to broaden what they teach so as to range beyond Christianity. Despite these developments non-Christian parents may still not feel satisfied with the religious education offered by their child's LEA school for the following reasons. First, parents might feel that although other faiths were being dealt with in classes on religious education, the vast bulk of the teaching still revolved around Christianity. Secondly, some parents might feel that the syllabus contained coverage of such a mixture of faiths that the whole course was too superficial and confusing to be of much value. It is well known, for example, that some Muslim parents are interested primarily in their children receiving rigorous instruction in the doctrines of Islam from a committed teacher, rather than in learning about religions in general as part of the overall curriculum. In these circumstances the parents can either withdraw the child completely from all religious education at school and make suitable arrangements for the child's instruction themselves, or else they can demand that the LEA make suitable alternative arrangements for instruction in the child's own faith. This can take place either at another school or elsewhere at the beginning or end of the school day or session. If the child is attending a LEA secondary school and suitable arrangements cannot conveniently be made for the child to receive separate tuition elsewhere, the LEA has an obligation to facilitate it at the child's own school, provided the cost does not fall upon the LEA and suitable arrangements can be made by the school itself. On the other hand, the LEA does not have to facilitate such separate instruction at the child's own school if it is a LEA primary school or a voluntary aided school. This is rather unsatisfactory because it means the child will have to go somewhere else for tuition. So far as voluntary aided schools are concerned, the expectation would generally be that the form of religious education offered would conform to the particular faith of the school concerned (eg Anglican, Roman Catholic or Jewish). A parent who does not want this may demand either separate instruction elsewhere or classes in accordance with the 'agreed syllabus' within the school itself, if the child cannot conveniently attend another school when such classes are being given.

The right of parents to withdraw children from the act of collective worship or classes of religious education (or both) is, in practice, exercised comparatively rarely, no doubt because it is somewhat embarrassing for children to be separated from their schoolmates in this manner. However, even those parents who do not wish to take this step may feel it important to make known to the school their feelings about religious education so that schools and LEAs become ever more responsive to the wishes of non-Christian parents.

How can an old-fashioned agreed syllabus be updated and revised?

Each LEA has a Standing Advisory Council on Religious Education (SACRE). This Council is made up of four committees representing the LEA, the teachers' associations, the Church of England, and other denominations reflecting the religious traditions of the area. The Council has a duty to monitor religious education in its area and it has the power to require the LEA to review its agreed syllabus if each of the committees other than the LEA votes in favour of this step being taken. Any new agreed syllabus must, under the terms of the Education Reform Act 1988, 'reflect the fact that the religious traditions in Great Britain are in the main Christian while taking account of the teaching and practices of the other principal religions represented in Great Britain'. Hence a proper place must be found for Buddhism, Hinduism, Islam, Judaism and Sikhism in all new syllabuses.

3 THE SECULAR CURRICULUM

Under the Education Act 1944 no particular subjects are laid down as compulsory parts of the 'secular' (non-religious) curriculum. Although all schools in fact teach English and mathematics, for example, there is no provision in the Act which states that they have to do so, nor any requirement that a pupil study any particular subject. When the Education Reform Act 1988 comes fully into operation, the position will change and a 'national curriculum' will be introduced, in terms of which pupils will have to study three 'core' subjects and seven 'foundation' subjects (as well as religious education). The core subjects are English, mathematics and science. The foundation subjects are history, geography, technology, music, art and physical education and in addition, for those aged 11 to 16, a modern foreign language approved by the Department of Education and Science. Pupils will be tested at certain specified ages (around 7, 11, 14 and 16) to see what level of achievement they have attained. How much time is devoted to each of the core and foundation subjects will be a matter for each individual school to decide, but together they are expected to take up about 70 per cent of the timetable for 14-16 year olds.

(a) Mother-tongue teaching

Many Asian parents would like their children to learn or maintain their 'mother-tongue', ie a language of their countries of origin, so that they can be bilingual. In this way the children can preserve a vital link with their cultural heritage as well as being able to communicate with relations who do not understand English. Sometimes classes in the various Asian languages are made available at state schools, but more frequently parents are left to arrange them privately on a voluntary basis at weekends or in the evenings. Despite the advantages for the children themselves of having these languages taught during normal school hours as part of the ordinary curriculum, there appears to be no legal duty upon schools or LEAs to organise the teaching of particular languages just because they are the 'mother-tongues' of many of their pupils. An EEC Directive issued in 1977 imposed a legal duty upon the member states of the European Communities to 'take appropriate measures to promote, in co-ordination with normal education, teaching of the mother-tongue', but this was aimed at the children of nationals of the other EEC countries, not those who are from the Indian subcontinent or are UK citizens. However, a number of Asian languages have been designated as 'foundation subjects' within the national curriculum by the Department of Education and Science. These are Arabic, Chinese, Hindi, Punjabi, Turkish, Bengali, Gujerati, Japanese and Urdu. These may be offered by schools, but only if the school also offers a major European language such as French, German, Italian or Spanish.

(b) Multicultural education

Asian parents are rightly concerned to ensure that there is no cultural bias in their children's schooling which might result in them failing to perform up to the level of their true abilities. Fortunately, many LEAs, schools and teachers have recently begun to appreciate the importance of a truly multicultural education in which the teaching, syllabus, textbooks and examinations reflect the diversity of the cultural backgrounds of the British population as a whole. Such an education not only helps to give Asian children a pride in their own cultural heritage but also enlightens white pupils about the nature of the wider society in which they are living today. From a practical point of view one of the most crucial ways in which multicultural education can be promoted and guaranteed is through public examination papers which do not contain any bias or discrimination against pupils from minority groups. Some of the examining boards have been criticised on this account in the past, but there are signs that a considerable advance in this respect has been made with the new GCSE syllabuses, assessments and examinations.

Any parents who are dissatisfied with their LEA on the basis of any cultural bias operating in its schools may like to remind the authority of its duty under the Race Relations Act 1976 to make appropriate arrangements with a view to securing that its various functions 'are carried out with due regard to the need —

(a) to eliminate unlawful discrimination;

and

(b) to promote equality of opportunity and good relations between persons of different racial groups.'

Where there is a cultural bias in the curriculum or the teaching, pupils are not being given equality of opportunity in fulfilling their true potential and achieving academic success. Furthermore, it is important to bear in mind the fact that the Education Reform Act 1988 lays a duty upon the Secretary of State for Education as well as all LEAs, governing bodies and headteachers, to ensure that the curriculum of each school is balanced and broadly based and in particular that it promotes the spiritual, moral and cultural development of the pupils at the school.

(c) Sex education

Schools do not have a duty to provide sex education as a matter of law, but many teachers feel it is part of their responsibility to do so. Some Asian parents are concerned that such teaching may have a corrupting influence on their children. They have formed a strong impression that white youngsters in Britain have loose morals and therefore are not good models for their own sons and daughters to follow. Under the Education (No 2) Act 1986, LEAs and school governors now have a duty to take such steps as are reasonably practicable to ensure that, where sex education is available to pupils, it is given 'in such a manner as to encourage those pupils to have due regard to moral considerations and the value of family life'. The result should be that teachers deal with sex education in a manner which sets it in the sort of context which most Asian parents would find acceptable. Furthermore, although parents have no legal right to withdraw their children from classes in sex education, school governors do have a discretion to allow such withdrawal and have been encouraged by the DES to exercise this discretion where parents have expressed strong religious objections to sex education at school.

4 APPROPRIATE DRESS FOR SCHOOL

Many Asian parents are keen to ensure that school rules and regulations in relation to their children's dress should fully respect their religious beliefs and cultural traditions. In particular they may well be concerned that their teenage daughters should not have to wear skirts as part of the school uniform, preferring instead the traditional *shalwar* (or trousers). Gym-slips, shorts and swimming costumes may also be unacceptable, especially to Muslim parents. Similarly some Sikh parents wish their sons to wear turbans to school.

Over the years there have been several much publicised disputes between schools and parents over such matters. Sometimes schools have tried to insist that all pupils wear exactly the same clothes as part of a standard uniform and have been unwilling to make concessions to Asian cultural and religious traditions. Fortunately, many schools have now liberalised their rules about dress generally and some LEAs have also issued guidelines on the subject to their schools, encouraging them to be more tolerant of diversity. An example of the latter is the model code on school clothing which was issued by Bradford Metropolitan Council to all its schools in 1982. This provided for the wearing of traditional dress (so long as it was in the school colours), the wearing of Sikh bracelets (on the basis that they do not constitute jewellery), and the wearing by girls of lightweight trousers for physical education classes and swimming lessons.

Moreover, in the light of an important court decision in 1983 it now seems unlikely that in future any school will refuse to admit an Asian pupil or send an Asian pupil home on the basis that the child is inappropriately dressed, simply because he or she is following a religious practice or cultural tradition. To do so without a very good reason would almost always involve a breach of the Race Relations Act 1976 and be unlawful. In the case of *Mandla v Dowell Lee* (1983) the House of Lords ruled firmly against a headmaster who refused to admit a Sikh boy as a pupil solely because the boy's parents wanted their son to wear a turban and the school regulations did not allow pupils to wear anything on their heads other than the school cap. The House of Lords held that such conduct on the part of the headmaster amounted to unlawful 'indirect discrimination' under the terms of the 1976 Act. The difficult concept of 'indirect discrimination' will be described in greater detail in chapter 12 in relation to employment (where it has the most practical relevance today), but a brief explanation is given here as to why the headmaster was found to be in the wrong. He set down a rule for pupils at his school, namely 'no headwear other than school caps' which, although it applied equally to all pupils (irrespective of their religion or race), nevertheless had an unfair effect upon one particular ethnic group (Sikhs) because far fewer of them can conscientiously comply with such a rule than others (ie non-Sikhs). Since wearing a turban is a religious requirement for orthodox Sikhs, they are much more harshly affected by such a rule than other groups and in that sense the rule indirectly discriminated against them. This idea should become clearer once chapter 12 has been studied, but the practical result is that any school which refuses to admit an Asian pupil because it objects to a form of dress which is required by religion or tradition, will be breaking the law, unless it can show that its regulation is 'justifiable'. The headmaster in *Mandla v Dowell Lee* failed to prove that his rule about not allowing any form of headwear (other than a school cap) was justifiable. He tried to justify the rule on two grounds — first, on the basis of its practical convenience, as part of a policy of trying to minimise external differences between pupils of different races and social classes and discourage competitive fashions among members of a teenage community; and secondly, on the ground that he wanted to project the image of a Christian school. Neither reason was accepted by the House of Lords. In the light of this decision, it seems hard to imagine that a school ban could lawfully be imposed upon Asian girls wearing *shalwar* or upon Muslim girls wearing *dupattas* (headscarves). Early in 1990 the head of a girls' grammar school in Cheshire suspended two Muslim pupils because they insisted on wearing their *dupattas*, but her decision was quickly reversed by the school's governors, no doubt at least partly in view of the provisions of the Race Relations Act. The head had initially sought to justify her suspension of the pupils on the grounds of health and safety (eg in the science laboratories), but photographs in the press revealed that the scarves worn by the girls were neatly tucked in and were not left freely flowing. By way of contrast, a school regulation which prohibited Sikh pupils from wearing *kirpans* or religious daggers (other than very small ones) might well be justifiable on the ground of the need to preserve the safety of all pupils. In 1983 a Sikh pupil in Leicester was suspended from his Sixth Form College for insisting upon wearing an eight-inch long *kirpan* and this would seem to have been perfectly justifiable.

5 SCHOOL MEALS

It is not only the refusal to admit a pupil which may amount to unlawful discrimination under the Race Relations Act 1976. It is also illegal for a school to discriminate against an existing pupil in the way it gives access to any benefits, facilities or services.

Does this mean that a school which only served pork at lunchtime on certain days would be acting unlawfully?

Yes, it might well be held to be practising unlawful indirect discrimination against Muslim pupils, unless it could show the system was justifiable. The school might try to justify its practice by indicating that it needed to run its meals service economically and efficiently, but it seems most unlikely that this would be a sufficient justification. In most schools there is a choice of menu and in many with a substantial number of Muslim students, *halal* meat is served.

6 CELEBRATION OF FESTIVALS

Under the Education Act 1944 pupils are entitled to be absent from school on any day exclusively set apart for religious observance by the religious body to which their parents belong. This means that, if their parents so wish, they can stay at home to celebrate the important religious festivals recognised by their particular faith.

Sometimes these festival days coincide with the dates of public examinations such as GCSE or 'A' levels. Parents or schools should notify the appropriate examining board well in advance if this is likely to happen and alternative arrangements can usually then be made. The normal practice is for the candidate affected either to sit the same examination paper on the day after the festival, subject to overnight supervision, or else to sit a different paper altogether at a different date.

CHAPTER 12

Employment

It is a deplorable yet undeniable fact that, despite considerable efforts on the part of both Parliament and the Commission for Racial Equality in recent years, there is still widespread racial discrimination in the field of employment in Britain.

Research findings published by the Policy Studies Institute in 1985 revealed that large numbers of Asian job applicants were being discriminated against solely on the basis of their colour or their origins. An experiment was conducted in which two equally well qualified candidates, one white and the other Asian, made preliminary inquiries, either in writing or over the telephone, about applying for a wide variety of different jobs in London, Birmingham and Manchester. Overall, whereas 90% of the white applicants received a positive response in the sense that they were offered interviews or were sent application forms, the figure for Asian applicants was only 63%. Over one-third of the employers surveyed were practising such discrimination. The survey also showed that there had been no reduction in the levels of such discrimination from the position ten years earlier. It should be emphasised that this sort of blatant discrimination at the very beginning of an applicant's search for work is merely one aspect of a much wider problem. Discrimination may occur at the interview stage, during the process of selection of successful candidates, within the workplace itself when a person has found employment and at the dismissal stage. It may operate through the deliberate actions of prejudiced individuals or occur through the employer following policies and practices which are themselves racially biased, even though the employer is not motivated by any ill-will towards minority groups.

Since this book is concerned with Asian traditions rather than merely with Asian origins, the focus of most of the following pages will be upon the ways in which English law handles any problems which may arise from Asian employees or job applicants following religious and cultural patterns of behaviour. Obvious examples relate to the dress and appearance of employees and whether they may take time off work for worship and prayer. However, a certain amount of background information must first be given about the basic structure of the provisions of English race relations legislation.

1 RACE RELATIONS LEGISLATION

The Race Relations Act 1976 attempts to prevent discrimination in the employment field in the following manner. It declares that it is unlawful for an employer to discriminate against either an applicant for a job or an existing employee. Such discrimination is not made a criminal offence, but a civil action can be brought before an Industrial Tribunal by the person against whom the discrimination has been practised. The Commission for Racial Equality may give advice and financial assistance to those who wish to bring such complaints against employers. If unlawful discrimination is proved, a Tribunal may order the employer to pay compensation (up to a maximum of £8,925) to cover loss of earnings and injured feelings and may also recommend that the employer take steps within a specified time limit to avoid or reduce the adverse effect of the discrimination upon the applicant. In practice the amount of compensation ordered for injury to feelings tends to be rather low (on average about £300) and in cases of 'indirect discrimination' (defined below) no compensation at all is payable if there was no intention on the part of the employer to treat the claimant unfavourably on racial grounds. Often the most important outcome of the case is a public declaration by the Tribunal that unlawful discrimination has occurred and this may often be sufficient to force the employer to cease discrimination in the future.

There are two categories of person who may bring a claim against an employer, namely those seeking work and existing employees. So far as the first category is concerned, namely job applicants, it is unlawful for the employer to discriminate —

(a)   by refusing the applicant a job;

(b)   by offering the applicant a job, but on worse terms than others; or

(c)   by making arrangements or organising procedures for recruitment which are themselves discriminatory (eg in advertisements for jobs).

So far as the second category is concerned, ie current employees, it is unlawful for an employer to discriminate against an employee —

(a)   in the terms of employment laid down (eg lower pay or longer hours);

(b)   in the way the employee is given access to opportunities for promotion, transfer or training (eg requiring him or her to serve for a longer period than others before being sent on a training programme or promoted to a higher grade);

(c)   in the way the employee is given access to other benefits, facilities or services, such as subsidised meals, company cars, holiday entitlements or sick pay schemes;

(d)   in refusing to afford the employee any access whatsoever to the opportunities or benefits mentioned above in (b) and (c); or

(e)   in dismissing the employee or subjecting the employee to any other detriment, eg harassment, racial abuse, demotion, suspension from duties or enforced transfer.

The unlawfulness of all these various actions on the part of an employer is dependent upon proof that there has been 'discrimination'. Such proof is often very difficult to establish in practice through a lack of sufficient evidence, with the result that many employers are never brought to account. Furthermore, the word 'discrimination' is defined in the Act in an extremely detailed, technical and complex manner which makes it hard for a person to know whether he or she might be able to bring a successful claim. Yet it is vital to appreciate what is covered by the definition and what is excluded. The Act states that a person is regarded as having discriminated against another in two rather different sets of circumstances. The *first* situation is generally referred to as 'direct discrimination' and occurs where one person treats another less favourably than others and does so on 'racial grounds'. 'Racial grounds' means on the grounds of 'colour, race, nationality or ethnic or national origins'. Some examples from cases successfully brought before various Industrial Tribunals should help to make this concept clearer and connect it with the forms of discrimination by employers outlined above.

In *Sanghera v United Counties Omnibus Company* (1985) the Industrial Tribunal found that the defendant company had unlawfully discriminated against Mr Sanghera, a Sikh, on racial grounds in refusing to offer him a job as a bus driver. He had 15 years' experience with other bus companies and each time he approached the defendant company for work he was told there were no vacancies at present and that he would be contacted later when any arose. However, he was never contacted and subsequently discovered that all the vacancies that had arisen had been filled by white drivers. The Tribunal ordered the defendant company to pay Mr Sanghera compensation and eventually they agreed to give him a job as well.

In *Aminzadeh v Israel Newton & Sons Ltd* (1985) Mr Aminzadeh, an Iranian, had qualifications as a welder. He went to a Job Centre and asked the receptionist to telephone the defendant company so as to arrange an interview. After the time for the interview had been fixed and while the receptionist was spelling out Mr Aminzadeh's name over the phone, Mr Newton stated that his company did not want any 'coloured' men. The Tribunal found the company had discriminated on racial grounds and awarded Mr Aminzadeh £150 for his injured feelings.

In *Sahota v London Brick Co Ltd* (1987) Mr Sahota, a well-educated man of Indian origin, was similarly held to have been the victim of racial discrimination. However, unlike Mr Sanghera and Mr Aminzadeh who were job applicants, Mr Sahota already had a job. His employers restricted his opportunities by failing to send him on a training course, although junior white staff with less experience than Mr Sahota had been sent; subsequently he was denied promotion, yet candidates who were white were promoted despite having less experience. The Tribunal awarded him £500 for injury to his feelings and ordered that he be considered for any suitable supervisory post which arose in future. The company was also told to adopt and implement an 'equal opportunities' policy and to ensure that there was no discrimination in the future.

In *Noone v North West Thames Regional Health Authority* (1988) the Health Authority was found to have unlawfully discriminated against Dr Noone, a very well qualified Sri Lankan pathologist, in failing to appoint her to a post as a consultant microbiologist at Ashford Hospital. The Industrial Tribunal found that the interview she was given was a sham and that the appointing committee had operated on the basis of biased reasoning verging on arbitrariness, in taking the view that because of her racial origins she would not 'fit in'. She was awarded £5,000 in compensation, though this was reduced to £3,000 on appeal.

The *second* situation described in the 1976 Act as unlawful is usually referred to as 'indirect discrimination' because it operates in a more subtle and less obvious fashion. It involves practices which appear at first sight to be perfectly satisfactory (because they apply the same requirements to everyone regardless of race or origins) but which, upon closer examination, turn out to have a disproportionately adverse effect upon minority groups. The definition o 'indirect discrimination' in the Act is extremely detailed and contains four distinct elements, all of which need to be established to the satisfaction of the Industrial Tribunal. These four ingredients are —

(i)   The application by one person (A) to another person (B) of a requirement or condition which A applies equally to persons not of the same racial group as B. (For example, A, the employer, imposes a requirement on B, a job applicant from Pakistan, which he also imposes equally on all applicants who are not Pakistanis, namely that every employee in the company of a certain grade must possess a pass in English language at 'O' level or an equivalent qualification in English).

(ii)   This requirement or condition is such that the proportion of persons of the same racial group as B who can comply with it is considerably smaller than the proportion of persons not of that racial group who can comply with it. (This element will be satisfied if it can be proved that far fewer persons of Pakistani origin can comply with the English language requirement mentioned above in comparison with non-Pakistanis).

(iii)   A cannot show the above requirement or condition to be justifiable irrespective of the colour, race, nationality or ethnic or national origins of B. (This would be satisfied if A was unable to put forward a satisfactory explanation of why the requirement was needed, eg those employees doing the particular job B had applied for did not in actual practice require this standard of English because they were only doing manual tasks, did not need to refer to detailed documents and only had to be able to read safety warning signs).

(iv)   The above requirement or condition is to the detriment (disadvantage) of B because B cannot comply with it (eg B is refused the job because of his or her inability to comply and thus suffers disadvantage through the rejection of his or her application).

The example of a requirement of English language qualifications provides a good illustration of the concept of 'indirect discrimination' because it shows how easily an apparently unobjectionable rule applied to people of all racial and ethnic groups can turn out to have discriminatory effects if it is used in relation to jobs where it is quite unnecessary. On the other hand, where special skills are required it is perfectly justifiable for an employer to impose minimum qualifications and members of minority groups cannot claim that discrimination has occurred under the 1976 Act, simply because their applications are rejected for lack of such qualifications.

A number of cases alleging indirect discrimination have been brought before Industrial Tribunals by Asian applicants who have specifically complained about the attitudes of employers towards their dress or appearance. In particular some Sikhs have faced problems in relation to long hair, beards and turbans and some Asian women have encountered difficulties with respect to their wish to wear *shalwar* (baggy trousers) rather than skirts. We can use these and other caes to illustrate how each of the four elements of indirect discrimination outlined above can be satisfied.

(i) The application of a standard requirement or condition applicable to all

Examples of such requirements are company rules which state that all female employees must wear skirts (eg as a uniform), that no male employees may wear beards, that no headwear be worn or that only the employers' specified headwear is permitted.

(ii) Only a considerably smaller proportion of the applicant's racial group can comply with the requirement

The question is whether a smaller 'proportion' can comply, not fewer people in terms of absolute numbers. Probably the difference has to be 20 per cent or greater to amount to a 'considerably' smaller proportion. The definition of 'racial group' given in the Act is 'a group of persons defined by reference to colour, race, nationality or ethnic or national origins'. It is noticeable that 'religion' is not mentioned in this definition and it is clear that the purpose of the 1976 Act was basically to prohibit racial discrimination, not religious discrimination. Hence Roman Catholics and members of Eastern Orthodox churches are obviously not protected by the definition of 'racial group' given above. However, some religious groups are also 'ethnic' groups and therefore do qualify for protection. In *Mandla v Dowell Lee* (1983), the facts of which were given in Chapter 11, the House of Lords defined what is meant by an 'ethnic group'. Lord Fraser declared —

> 'For a group to constitute an ethnic group it must regard itself, and be regarded by others as a distinct community by virtue of certain characteristics. Some of these are essential; others are not essential but one or more will commonly be found and will help to distinguish the group from the surrounding community.'

The two conditions Lord Fraser held to be essential were, first, a long shared history, of which the group is conscious as distinguishing it from other groups, and the memory of which keeps it alive; and secondly, a cultural tradition of its own, including family and social customs and manners, often but not necessarily associated with religious observance. The other non-essential but very relevant characteristics of ethnicity mentioned by Lord Fraser were —

(a)   either a common geographical origin or descent from a small number of common ancestors;

(b)   a common language, not necessarily peculiar to the group;

(c)   a common literature peculiar to the group;

(d)   a common religion different from that of neighbouring groups or from the general community surrounding it; and

(e)   being a minority or being an oppressed or a dominant group within a larger community.

It is clear from the case of *Mandla v Dowell Lee* that both Sikhs and Jews are entitled to be regarded as ethnic as well as religious groups, but it has yet to be decided by the courts whether Muslims, Hindus, Buddhists or Jains qualify. Would it be accurate to say that each of these groups had a *'shared'* history which distinguishes it from other groups? Muslims, for example, are found in sizeable numbers in many different parts of the world (eg the USSR and West Africa) where their historical experiences have been rather different. Although Hindus clearly have had a shared history in India, do they regard it as distinguishing them from the other communities there? Similarly would it be right to say that each group has a cultural tradition 'of its own'? The family and social customs of Muslims surely differ to some degree, depending upon whether they are living in the Middle East, the Indian subcontinent, in Africa or in Europe. Despite these difficult points of interpretation of the meaning of 'ethnic group', it is perfectly possible that in a future case a court might decide that each of the above-mentioned religious groups was meant to be included, partly because it would be regarded as an odd result if Sikhs and Jews were 'counted in' and the others excluded.

In *Raval v DHSS* (1985) it was accepted by the Employment Appeal Tribunal that a woman of Asian origin who was born and brought up in Kenya could be regarded as being a member of an 'Asian racial group' and a person could obviously claim to be a member of a distinct racial group on the basis of Indian, Pakistani, Bangladeshi or Sri Lankan origins, because 'national origins' are within the Act's definition of 'racial group'. The Act also states that 'the fact that a racial group comprises two or more distinct racial groups does not prevent it from constituting a particular racial group for the purposes of this Act.'

The question whether a considerably smaller proportion of the applicant's racial group can comply with the employer's requirement involves an interpretation of the words 'can comply'. If a company has a rule that no employee may wear a beard, can an orthodox Sikh comply with it? Physically he could because he could shave off his beard, but in *Mandla v Dowell Lee* the House of Lords stated that the words 'can comply' must not be interpreted literally but as meaning 'can in practice' or 'can consistently with the customs and cultural conditions of the racial group'. Similarly, Asian women can physically wear skirts, but many of them cannot comply with a 'no trousers' rule consistently with their cultural traditions and religious beliefs. In one case the judge said the

99

question should be decided taking into account 'the current usual behaviour of women in this respect, as observed in practice, putting on one side behaviour or responses which are unusual or extreme.'

(iii) The employer cannot show the requirement to be justifiable

A number of different types of justification have been put forward by employers and there has been some disagreement in the decisions of courts and tribunals as to the correct meaning of the word 'justifiable'.

In *Singh v Rowntree Mackintosh Ltd* (1979) and *Panesar v Nestlé Co Ltd* (1980) the applicants were orthodox Sikhs who had been refused employment at factories manufacturing sweets and chocolates because the companies in question had rules prohibiting the wearing of beards at these factories. The applicants could not in practice comply with these rules and it was taken for granted in the proceedings that the proportion of Sikhs who could conscientiously comply with the rules was considerably smaller than the proportion of non-Sikhs who could do so. The only issue, therefore, became whether the rules were justifiable. The companies argued that beards could not be allowed in their factories for reasons of hygiene; small particles or hairs might fall into bars of chocolate as they were being made. In both cases they were successful, mainly because the tribunals believed they were entitled to try to attain very high standards of hygiene in the interests of public health and the protection of consumers.

By way of contrast, an orthodox Sikh was successful in a claim against a different chocolate manufacturer in *Kamaljeet Singh Bhakerd v Famous Names Ltd* (1988). The employers had a rule which required all their employees to wear caps provided by the company which were kept on their premises and laundered by them. The applicant was refused a job by the company because he wanted to wear a turban rather than a company cap. The Industrial Tribunal ruled that the company's requirement was unjustifiable because the same high standards of hygiene could be achieved equally well by allowing Sikhs to wear turbans as by insisting that they wore company caps. Both would be equally good at preventing hair falling into the chocolates. The company could easily make a special arrangement for Sikhs and if necessary insist that turbans used in the factory were laundered on the company's premises and regularly inspected for cleanliness. The convenience of the employer's rule did not mean that it was justifiable and the company was therefore found to have unlawfully discriminated against the applicant.

In *Kuldip Singh v British Rail Engineering Ltd* (1985) the applicant was an orthodox Sikh who was employed as a railway carriage repair worker. He always wore a turban. After he had been working for BREL for about 12 years (without accident or injury) a new production controller became concerned about safety standards in the applicant's section and decided to introduce the wearing of hard hats or 'bump caps'. He was concerned to protect employees from the danger of falling tools and from any risk of injury if they banged their heads on the underside of the railway carriages. The applicant refused to wear a 'bump cap' in place of his turban and as a result was demoted to a position where bump caps were not required. He alleged indirect discrimination, but the company was held to be acting lawfully because its rule about bump caps was justifiable on grounds of safety. If the rule had not been enforced, the company might have been sued or prosecuted for not taking proper care of its employees' health in this regard.

In *Kingston and Richmond Area Health Authority v Kaur* (1981) the applicant was a Sikh woman who wanted to train as a nurse and who had been accepted onto a two-year course by the health authority. When the authority later discovered that she intended to continue wearing *shalwar-qemiz* (a long shirt or tunic worn over baggy trousers) upon qualifying as a nurse, the authority withdrew their offer of a training place on the ground that all nurses had to wear a standard uniform consisting of a dress or a frock. The Industrial Tribunal before which she brought her claim of indirect discrimination accepted that a considerably smaller proportion of Sikh, Punjabi or Indian women could comply with the rule about nurses' uniforms than the proportion of other women not of those 'racial' groups. It found that around 60-70 per cent of Sikh women living in the UK wore *shalwar-qemiz* as a cultural or religious requirement. It did not consider the rule about uniform to be justifiable. However, it was overruled on this last point by the Employment Appeal Tribunal (EAT). The EAT discovered that to a large degree the rigid rules about nurses' uniforms were laid down by the General Nursing Council in regulations made under an Act of Parliament and this contributed to its decision that they were justifiable. However, strong pressure was then placed upon the General Nursing Council by the DHSS to revise its rules about dress and the new rules made in 1981 are very flexible. In consequence, Miss Kaur was once again offered a training place by the Kingston and Richmond Health Authority on the understanding that when she had qualified as a nurse she would wear grey *shalwar* and a white *qemiz*.

In *Malik v British Home Stores* (1980) the applicant, a Muslim schoolgirl aged 18, had been refused employment by BHS in its Bradford store because it operated a rule requiring all female sales staff to wear skirts and she had insisted, on religious grounds, upon wearing clothing which fully covered her legs. BHS attempted to justify the rule to the Industrial Tribunal on the basis that commercial necessity dictated that all its shop assistants should wear a uniform and that the image of its stores required that their uniform rules should be kept to in all branches across the country. The Tribunal rejected this argument, pointing out that only a small alteration to the uniform was required to accommodate the needs of Muslim women and that Muslims might well account for as many as 14 per cent of BHS customers in Bradford. After declaring that BHS had acted unlawfully, the Tribunal specifically recommended that within 28 days of its decision BHS should alter its rules about uniform so that Muslim women of Pakistani origin could wear a uniform which incorporated *shalwar*. Four years later Woolworths also amended its 'skirts only' rule to meet the needs of Asian women, following the settlement out of court of a claim against them by a woman of Bangladeshi origin who had been refused a job as a sales assistant in Northampton.

So far as the correct technical interpretation of the word 'justifiable' is concerned, it is only possible to say at present that there have been a variety of different views expressed in the decided cases. Clearly an employer cannot justify a rule that is discriminatory simply on the basis of a whim or business convenience or the ease of following established practices and procedures. In one case the judge indicated that reasons 'which would be acceptable to right-thinking people as sound and tolerable reasons' would be sufficient to render a requirement justifiable. In *Kuldip Singh v British Rail Engineering Ltd* the EAT stated that justifiable did not mean 'necessary' and that it would be sufficient if the reasons given were 'good or adequate'. However, in other cases the trend has been towards following American rulings which have explained that the requirement should be objectively necessary, that it should be closely related to the job to which it is being applied and that there should be no other reasonable and satisfactory way of achieving the employer's objectives. American decisions are particularly relevant here because the concept of indirect discrimination in English law was modelled upon U.S. case law. The imposition of a test of 'objective necessity' would bring English law into line not only with comparable decisions of the U.S. Supreme Court but also with the standard set for religious freedom in the European Convention of Human Rights, as well as a ruling about EEC law in the European Court of Justice in 1986 on indirect discrimination in the closely related field of sexual equality. If such a test is indeed the correct one, as many commentators now argue, then some of the previous decisions on this point may not accurately represent the current state of English law. The rules adopted by the employers in *Singh v Rowntree Mackintosh, Panesar v Nestlé Co Ltd* and *Kuldip Singh v British Rail Engineering Ltd* were probably not justifiable under this test because the hygiene and safety risks were not really very great and there might well have been satisfactory alternative methods of tackling the problems there without having to discriminate indirectly against Sikhs. Beards, for instance, can be neatly covered by face masks or nets known as 'snoods'. Even surgeons are allowed to have beards but they wear suitable clothing to prevent infection while they perform operations. Similarly, protective headwear can sometimes be worn over a lightweight turban by those engaged in hazardous activities and with this in mind special helmets have occasionally been manufactured for Sikh riders, jockeys and airmen. The point here is that although the employers' arguments in these cases about their rules being justifiable upon grounds of health and safety were plausible, closer examination suggests that the rules were not absolutely necessary. The standards demanded by the employers could probably have been maintained in other ways and this factor is important when it is placed in the context of a practice which has the effect of discriminating exclusively against Sikhs.

(iv) The requirement is to the detriment of the applicant because he or she cannot comply with it

The purpose of this element is merely to emphasise that the applicants have to show that they themselves have suffered a disadvantage in not being able to satisfy the requirement. They have to prove that they themselves have been victims of indirect discrimination in being denied something available to others.

Are there special rules about the wearing of headgear on construction sites?

Yes. As from 1990 it is compulsory for virtually all persons working on construction sites to wear suitable head protection in the form of a safety helmet. This new rule is contained in the Construction (Head Protection) Regulations 1989. However, a specific exemption from this requirement has been created for turbanned Sikhs by the Employment Act 1989. Furthermore, any employer who refuses to employ a turbanned Sikh on a construction site simply because he is unwilling to wear a safety helmet in place of his turban, will be barred from being able to argue that such a policy is justifiable on grounds of safety under the indirect discrimination provisions of the Race Relations Act. There are estimated to be around 40,000 Sikhs employed in the construction industry and these exemptions were felt by Parliament to be necessary both to protect their jobs and to preserve religious freedom. One consequence of the exemptions is that if a turbanned Sikh is injured on a construction site as a result of the negligent act of another person, the Sikh may only claim 'damages' (monetary compensation) from the person at fault for any injuries that would have been suffered even if he had been wearing a safety helmet. The law thus takes the view that the Sikh should be regarded as partly responsible for such an injury, having taken an extra risk by not wearing a safety helmet. It should also be borne in mind that these rules only apply to 'construction sites' and not, for example, to engineering workshops such as the British Rail one where Kuldip Singh worked (see above). For the purposes of the Employment Act 1989, a construction site means any place where any 'building operations' or 'works of engineering construction' are being undertaken. 'Building operations' means the construction, structural alteration, repair, maintenance or demolition of a building or the laying of any foundations. 'Works of engineering construction' include the construction, structural alteration, repair and demolition of docks, harbours, tunnels, bridges, waterworks and gasholders.

Are there any exceptions to the rules banning unlawful discrimination in the field of employment?

Very few. The provisions of the Race Relations Act protect not only job applicants and employees but also those seeking to become partners in firms of solicitors, accountants and other professions (so long as there are six or more partners), those wishing to join trade unions or employers' organisations, those seeking enrolment in qualifying bodies (such as the British Medical Association or the Law Society), those applying for places on vocational training courses and those wanting to use the services of an employment agency.

In the context of the present discussion there are, however, five main exceptions where the Act's provisions banning discrimination do not apply. They are —

(a)   Employment in a private household.

(b)   Employment outside Great Britain.

(c)   Acts done under statutory authority, ie done to comply with an Act of Parliament or in pursuance of a statutory regulation or in compliance with a condition or requirement imposed by a government Minister. An example of this would be a statutory regulation which made it compulsory in certain types of dangerous work to wear a helmet (eg blasting operations with dynamite). Here an employer who refused to allow a Sikh merely to wear a turban would simply be able to rely on this exception and would not need to prove the discrimination was 'justifiable' (as explained above).

(d)   Genuine occupational qualifications. One example of this is where the job involves participation in a dramatic performance or entertainment in a capacity for which a person of a particular racial group is required for reasons of authenticity. Thus a Chinese man could not claim unlawful discrimination if he was refused employment by an African dance troupe as one of their performers on stage. Another example under this heading is where the holder of a particular job provides persons of a specific racial group with personal services promoting their welfare, and those services can most effectively be provided by a person from that racial group. Hence it would be lawful to reject a white applicant if the job was one of providing advice and assistance to Asian women who were being ill-treated by their husbands.

(e)   Special needs. It is not unlawful for an employer to afford persons of a particular racial group access to facilities or services to meet the special needs of persons of that group in regard to their education, training and welfare or any related benefits. Hence it would not be unlawful, for example, for an employer who had Muslim employees to set aside a special room in his premises in which prayers could be said or for a company which employed a number of workers from Bangladesh whose ability to read English was very limited, to provide them with special English language classes.

Are there any time-limits for bringing claims about discrimination to an Industrial Tribunal?

Yes, normally any claim must be made within 3 months of the act of discrimination alleged, though this time limit may occasionally be extended by the Tribunal if it feels it would be just to do so.

Apart from the 1976 Act has Parliament made any attempt to encourage employers to adopt attitudes and practices which respect Asian traditions?

In 1983 Parliament approved a 'Code of Practice' on Race Relations which had been prepared by the Commission for Racial Equality. It was brought into force on 1st April 1984. The Code sets out guidance for employers about practices which are recommended with a view to eliminating discrimination in employment and promoting equal opportunity. It does not have the force of law, so failure to follow its guidelines is not itself unlawful. However, its provisions may be taken into account by any tribunal or court hearing a case on discrimination and thus failure to observe the Code may lead to a presumption that there has been unlawful discrimination.

The Code contains the following statement —

'Where employees have particular cultural and religious needs which conflict with existing work requirements, it is recommended that employers should consider whether it is reasonably practicable to vary or adapt these requirements to enable such needs to be met. For example, it is recommended that they should not refuse employment to a turbanned Sikh because he could not comply with unjustifiable uniform requirements.'

In practice many employers now find no difficulty in allowing turbans. Blue ones are permitted in the police force in place of helmets, blue and yellow ones are worn by traffic wardens, green ones are worn by tennis umpires and linesmen at Wimbledon, khaki ones are permitted in the Army and white ones are accepted in place of wigs for barristers and judges.

The Code also mentions three other cultural or religious needs which employers should consider attempting to accommodate, namely the wearing of saris or *shalwar-qemiz* by Asian women, the observance of prayer times by Muslims and the observance of religious holidays. The first of these has already been examined and so attention will now be turned to the second and third.

2   THE OBSERVANCE OF PRAYER TIMES BY MUSLIMS

The five obligatory daily prayers for Muslims are scheduled at dawn (*fajr*), early afternoon (*zuhr*), late afternoon (*asr*), sunset (*maghrib*) and late evening (*isha*). A number of Muslim organisations in Britain produce regular prayer timetables indicating exact times for these five prayers, but these primarily relate to congregational prayers by worshippers in mosques, and for those not attending, eg those who are at work, there is a great deal of flexibility, at least for those who are not ultra-orthodox and rigid in their beliefs. It should prove possible, in most cases, for Muslim employees to arrange to fit their prayers into tea-breaks or the lunch-hour without any difficulty. Sensible employers will provide washing facilities and perhaps even a separate room for congregational *zuhr* prayers on Fridays.

A Muslim who is inflexible in his attitude to prayer times may find that he is dismissed perfectly lawfully by his employer for failure to carry out his work according to the duties laid down in his contract. In the case of *Hussain v London Country Bus Services Ltd* (1984) Mr Hussain had been employed by the bus company to clean buses and coaches. He worked on the early evening shift when there was often pressure to clean the buses quickly and return them to service. However, he insisted upon breaking off work at this time for *maghrib* prayers and his absences caused problems both for the company and for the other employees. Although Mr Hussain was acknowledged by the company to be a good and productive worker who made up for his absences for prayer later in the evening, the company eventually decided it had to dismiss him. The Industrial Tribunal decided that the dismissal had not been unfair and therefore Mr Hussain was not entitled to claim any compensation for the loss of his job. The Tribunal ruled that if he was going to insist on rigid observance of sunset prayers regardless of the pressures of work, he should have made this clear to the company from the start of his employment. The company had indicated that they had no objection to him praying during meal breaks or tea breaks and the Tribunal felt that the company's attitude had not been unreasonable. Obviously the best way of sorting out problems of this kind is for an agreement to be reached between employer and employee at the beginning of the contract. Many employers operate a 'flexi-time' system under which a specified number of hours have to be worked each week but the employee is to some extent free to decide when those hours should be fitted in. The difficulty, of course, with the London Country Bus Service was that they needed certain types of work to be done at very specific times.

Another example of a Muslim failing in his claim for compensation for 'unfair dismissal' under the Employment Protection (Consolidation) Act 1978 is the case of *Ahmad v Inner London Education Authority* (1978). Mr Ahmad, who was born in India, was employed by ILEA as a full-time schoolteacher. During the years 1968-1974 the schools where he worked were too far away from a mosque for him to attend *zuhr* prayers on Fridays, but when in 1974 he was transferred to a school only about fifteen or twenty minutes' walk away from a mosque he began regular attendance at Friday prayers. This meant that since the school's lunch-break ran from 12.30 to 1.30 pm and the *zuhr* prayers lasted till 2.00 pm, he arrived back at school roughly 45 minutes after lessons had re-started. This caused some resentment among his fellow teachers and eventually (after several warnings) the ILEA told him that if he wished to continue this practice he should give up his full-time contract and be appointed for only a four and a half day week, with a consequent reduction in salary. Rather than accept this, Mr Ahmad resigned and subsequently claimed compensation and re-employment as a full-time teacher. His claim failed despite appeals both to the English Court of Appeal and to the European Commission on Human Rights. The main principles to emerge from the case were that —

(i) an employee cannot break his contractual duties simply on the ground that he is practising his religion;

(ii) schools ought to try to arrange their timetables so that Muslims are able to observe prayer times, but they cannot be compelled to do so; and

(iii) the rights of the employer, the pupils and the other teachers must be borne in mind fully in cases of this sort.

The final result, namely that Mr Ahmad was held to have been fairly dismissed, may seem harsh to some people. Indeed in the Court of Appeal, Lord Scarman disagreed with the other two judges and believed the dismissal was unfair. He was very concerned lest Muslims who took their religious duties seriously could never become full-time schoolteachers and would always have to be given part-time appointments. He felt that an absence of 45 minutes per week for Friday prayers should not prevent the grant of a full-time post. He considered that education authorities should make suitable administrative arrangements to ensure that the pupils were taught and that other teachers were not unfairly burdened. This might mean employing a few more teachers, but this cost would be small in comparison with other public expenditure already considered appropriate in the interest of fighting discrimination. However, it is important to remember that Lord Scarman was in the minority and also that Mr Ahmad failed to prove to the satisfaction of the European Commission on Human Rights that he had been the victim of a violation of the European Convention and that he had been denied the right to freedom of religion. Furthermore, it was clear from the case that the vast majority of Muslim teachers in English schools do not claim the right to be absent from their classes on Fridays. They interpret the requirements of their religion flexibly or else are able to reach a satisfactory agreement with their employers about their timetables.

What exactly does an employee have to show in order to succeed in a claim for 'unfair dismissal'?

Under the terms of the Employment Protection (Consolidation) Act 1978 a dismissal will be held to be unfair unless the employer can prove first, that it occurred wholly or mainly because of the employee's incapacity, misconduct, breach of statutory duty, redundancy 'or other substantial reason' and secondly, that in all the circumstances the employer acted reasonably and fairly in treating this particular ground as a sufficient reason for dismissal in the individual case. The second question has to be decided on the basis of the facts known to the employer at the moment of dismissal and usually the employee will need to have been given advance warning of any allegations of misconduct or incapacity and an opportunity to rectify the position or explain his side of the story. Claims for unfair dismissal can only be brought by those who had worked for the employer who dismissed them for a continuous period of at least one year.

A case in which a Sikh's dismissal was held by the Industrial Tribunal to be perfectly fair was *Singh v Lyons Maid Ltd* (1975). The claimant was engaged in the manufacture of ice-cream at the respondent's factory. When he was initially recruited he was clean-shaven. The company had a rule, of which he was very well aware, that beards were not allowed to be worn by staff on the production floor for reasons of hygiene. However, when he returned from a holiday during the seventh year of his employment with the company, he was wearing a beard. He announced that he had undergone a spiritual revival and wished to keep his beard for religious reasons. However, the company ordered him to shave it off and when, after repeated demands, he still refused to do so the company dismissed him. The Tribunal held that the rule banning beards on the production floor was part of his contract and a reasonable one in the interests of maintaining high standards of hygiene. His refusal to abide by it gave the company a good reason for sacking him and they had not acted unfairly in doing so.

If Mr Ahmad had brought a claim against the ILEA for 'indirect discrimination' instead of 'unfair dismissal' would he have won?

He might have done. We can test his claim against the four ingredients of 'indirect discrimination' outlined earlier.

(i)   There was certainly a standard requirement which applied to all ILEA teachers at his school, namely that they be available for classes from 1.30 pm onwards on Friday afternoons.

(ii)   Was it true that only a considerably smaller proportion of Mr Ahmad's racial group could conscientiously comply with this requirement than those not of his racial group? If it is assumed that his own racial group consisted of Muslims, or of people of Indian origin or even perhaps of Asians, this condition might well be satisfied.

(iii)   Could the ILEA show that the requirement was justifiable? If the meaning given to 'justifiable' by Industrial Tribunals around 1978 is used, then perhaps the ILEA could have shown this. However, if the new test of 'objective necessity' were to be chosen instead, then this is far more doubtful because there were surely other ways in which ILEA schools could have organised their timetables so as to accommodate attendance at *zuhr* prayer on Fridays.

(iv)   Was the requirement a detriment to Mr Ahmad because he could not comply with it? Undoubtedly it was, because it meant he lost his job as a full-time teacher.

If an individual who has suffered discrimination decides not to pursue a claim against an employer, can the Commission for Racial Equality take proceedings instead?

In practice very few individuals proceed with complaints of discrimination against employers. To do so requires a great deal of strength of character, patience and resilience and the final outcome is rarely satisfactory. The vast majority of claims are dismissed by the tribunals for lack of proof or on technical grounds and, even where a claimant succeeds, only small sums of compensation are ordered in direct discrimination cases and usually no compensation at all is payable in indirect discrimination cases. However, the CRE does not, unfortunately, have the right to take over the proceedings in order to establish the truth and uphold the point of principle. Its powers are strictly limited. Apart from assisting applicants who pursue their own individual claims, the CRE may independently conduct a 'formal investigation' into the practices of a specific employer where it has reasonable grounds for believing these to be discriminatory and, if it actually uncovers such discrimination, it may then issue a 'non-discrimination notice'. Such a notice may require the employer to cease the discriminatory practices and it can be enforced by means of a court order. However, this procedure is a very complicated one in practice and is rarely used by the CRE. It is not simply a matter of the CRE being able to take up a case of discrimination on behalf of an individual victim who lacks the energy to take proceedings himself: this is something which the CRE is not, at present, permitted to do.

3 ANNUAL FESTIVALS AND HOLIDAYS

English law recognises a number of Christian festivals in a special way by declaring that they are public holidays, but no Asian festivals are marked in this way. However, the status of a particular date as a public holiday does not mean that all employees are automatically entitled to take this day off work. Technically, only bank officials and a few other workers are guaranteed this right (hence the name 'bank holidays'). For other employees their rights are to be found in their individual contracts. Obviously in most cases they do not have to work on public holidays, but certain essential services still have to be maintained and today many people employed in shops and the entertainment industry are expected to work on these days. In the light of these principles it is clear that the rights of Muslims, Hindus, Sikhs and Buddhists to take days off work to celebrate particular festivals basically depend upon what arrangements are agreed with their employers. Some employers may allow such days to be taken out of annual holiday entitlement, others may permit absences in return for extra hours worked (eg on a public holiday), while a few may be prepared to grant extra days off for religious festivals. On the other hand, if employees have not managed to negotiate any entitlement and take days off without authorisation, they may well find that deductions have been made from their pay in respect of these absences. However, it is possible that such action on the part of an employer may constitute indirect discrimination and hence be unlawful. This depends upon whether or not each of the four ingredients of such discrimination can be satisfied, as follows —

(i)   There must be a standard requirement that all employees, regardless of their racial origins, work on a particular day, eg the Muslim festival of *Eid-al-Adha.*

(ii)   It must be shown that a considerably smaller proportion of Muslims than non-Muslims can conscientiously comply with this requirement. This should not be difficult to prove.

(iii)   The requirement must be unjustifiable. The employee would have to establish that there were acceptable ways in which the work which Muslims would have done on this day could have been re-allocated to other employees or else re-scheduled for another time. In the majority of cases it would probably be very hard for an employer to succeed in showing that refusing Muslim workers time off for the festival was justifiable.

(iv)   The requirement is obviously a detriment because it means that Muslims either lose a day's pay if they absent themselves or else they are deprived of the opportunity to celebrate a religious festival.

What is the position where an employee wishes to take an extended holiday in order to visit relations in the Indian subcontinent?

As we have seen, holiday entitlements are a matter to be agreed upon between employer and employee and form part of the contract between them. Often special arrangements can be made to allow employees to save up and accumulate their annual holiday entitlements so as to enable them to take extended leave overseas. Alternatively a period of unpaid leave may be granted. The Code of Practice warns employers to operate whatever policies they have in regard to extended periods of leave without unlawful discrimination and obviously it would be a breach of the Race Relations Act if white employees wishing to visit relatives in Australia or South Africa were given preferential treatment over Asian employees wanting to travel to the Indian subcontinent. However, there has been a growing practice among employers to ask those employees taking extended leave to sign a document stating that they agree to return on a specific date and that if they fail to do so they will be deemed to have terminated their employment. This tough stand taken by employers has been challenged by employees. In the case of *British Leyland (UK) Ltd v Ashraf* (1978) the applicant had been granted five weeks' unpaid leave in order to visit Pakistan when his mother was seriously ill. He returned late because he himself fell ill during the five week period. The company claimed that his employment had automatically terminated when he failed to return on the date specified in the document he had signed and the Employment Appeal Tribunal agreed with this conclusion. This meant that he could not claim compensation for unfair dismissal because he had not been 'dismissed'. However, in *Igbo v Johnson, Matthey Chemicals Ltd* (1986) the Court of Appeal ruled in a similar type of case that the decision of the Employment Appeal Tribunal in *Ashraf's* case had been wrong. This means that, in future, employees will not be prevented from claiming for unfair dismissal if they return late from a period of overseas leave and are told that their jobs have been terminated. Any agreement they have signed to the effect that they will automatically lose their employment if they fail to return on a given day will be ignored by tribunals and courts in future cases.

CHAPTER 13

Religious worship and observance

Religious toleration and freedom of worship are today greatly cherished values in English society. Religious minorities, such as Roman Catholics and Jews, did, of course, experience persecution and legal discrimination in the past and it is only since the middle of the 19th century that English law has contained provisions designed to safeguard religious freedom for all.

The UK is party to two international treaties which contain guarantees of freedom of religion, namely the European Convention on Human Rights and the International Covenant on Civil and Political Rights. The European Convention requires all contracting states, without discrimination, to guarantee to everyone freedom of 'thought, conscience and religion' and the right 'either alone or in community with others and in public or private, to manifest his religion or belief in worship, teaching, practice or observance' (article 9).

The English courts are not bound to apply the terms of the European Convention in the cases which come before them because the Convention is not, strictly speaking, a part of English law. The judges do, however, often take the provisions of the Convention into account in reaching their decisions because they do not want the UK to be held to be in breach of international law if a case is later brought before the European Commission of Human Rights or the European Court of Human Rights in Strasbourg. Individuals are permitted to bring legal proceedings against the British Government for violations of the Convention by petitioning the European Commission on Human Rights, provided they have first tried every practicable legal remedy available under English law in the English courts and still been unsuccessful. The European Commission then gives a preliminary ruling on the issue and the final decision is usually taken by the European Court, whose verdict is binding on the Government.

However, it needs to be borne in mind that the Convention does not provide an absolute guarantee of freedom of religion. One of its articles allows the state to impose legal limitations upon the manifestation of this freedom to the extent that these 'are necessary in a democratic society in the interests of public safety, for the protection of public order, health or morals, or for the protection of the rights and freedoms of others'. This affords the state a variety of grounds upon which it can justify placing restrictions, not upon a person's religious beliefs themselves but merely upon their manifestation or display in practice.

1   ACQUISITION OF PLACES OF WORSHIP

A building which is intended for use as a place of worship can be acquired in the name of an individual, a group of persons or a religious trust or foundation. A trust whose main purpose is the advancement (promotion) of religion qualifies as a 'charitable' trust in the eyes of the law and such trusts are entitled to a number of tax privileges which makes them particularly desirable.

Places of worship for use by adherents to Islam, Hinduism, Sikhism and Buddhism are usually acquired in one of the three ways outlined below.

(a) **Purpose-built**

The religious group or organisation acquires a vacant plot of land upon which the building is to be erected. Planning permission must be obtained from the local authority before work commences and this may be refused on a number of grounds or only granted upon certain conditions. It may well, therefore, be prudent not to complete the purchase of a site until it is clear that the necessary permission will be granted. Decisions about planning permission can often take a long time, especially if there are objections from local residents, and delays of well over 12 months are not uncommon. Among the many factors which the local authority planning committee takes into account are its own development plan for the area, the physical appearance of the proposed building, its likely impact upon the neighbourhood in terms of noise level, traffic flow and car parking facilities, and local issues of social and economic policy such as racial integration. All faiths are entitled to receive equal treatment, ie there must be no discrimination against particular religions. An increasing number of purpose-built mosques, temples and *gurdwaras* have appeared in English towns and cities in recent years.

(b) Acquisitions from other faiths

The purchase of a religious building from another faith is often a very satisfactory way of proceeding because planning permission is not required. During the course of the present century many churches have become redundant through the decline in public worship among the majority community, many of whom no longer regard themselves as being more than merely nominally Christian. Sales of churches by denominations other that the Church of England have been occurring for several years and recently the Anglican Church indicated that it was prepared to follow suit. A striking example of a building which has served a number of different religious faiths is the present London Jamme Masjid in Spitalfields in London's East End. It was built as a Huguenot (French Protestant) Church in 1744, was used as a Jewish synagogue from 1898 to 1975 and is now a mosque.

(c) Conversions of other buildings

A common practice has been to convert premises used for non-religious purposes (such as a school, a business or a dwelling house) into a mosque, a temple or a *gurdwara*. Sometimes two adjoining houses are converted into a single building for this purpose. This procedure does, however, involve obtaining prior planning permission and delays may therefore be expected. If the property is in a residential area, the planning authority may be particularly concerned about the likely size of the congregation and anxious about noise levels, the flow of traffic and parking problems. Since many worshippers regard it as spiritually beneficial and meritorious to walk to their place of worship rather than drive to it, undue concern about traffic and parking is often misplaced and this point should be drawn to the attention of the planning department.

What is the legal sanction if a person neglects to apply for planning permission when he should have done so?

A person who erects a building when he should not have done so can be compelled to demolish it, but someone who simply starts work without the necessary planning permission will commonly be told to make an immediate application for the relevant permission. In the meantime he will have to stop further activity and wait for the decision of the planning authority. Failure to do so after the issue of an 'enforcement notice' by the authority may result in a substantial fine being imposed under the Town and Country Planning Act 1971.

A person who uses an existing building as a place of worship without obtaining permission to change its use from a non-religious building to a religious one can similarly be ordered to cease doing so by the issue of an enforcement notice. If he fails to comply with such a notice he too will be liable to a substantial fine under the 1971 Act.

Appeals may be made against a refusal of planning permission or against the imposition of unreasonable conditions to the Secretary of State for the Environment. Often a government-appointed inspector will then make the decision or else a public inquiry will be held at which members of the public may express their opinions and be cross-examined as witnesses.

Are planning authorities willing to allow minarets to be built next to mosques so that the traditional 'call to prayer' can be proclaimed from the top?

In recent years a number of minarets have been erected (eg in London, Birmingham and Halifax) after the necessary planning permission had been obtained. Usually a condition has been imposed that the 'call to prayer' should not be amplified electronically through loudspeakers so as not to cause undue disturbance to nearby residents who are not Muslims. However, occasionally loudspeakers have been allowed, eg for the call to prayer at midday, with strict limits being placed upon the volume of noise permitted.

What happens if local residents complain about the noise caused by the call to prayer?

If the noise level is so great as to interfere substantially with the ordinary comfort of neighbours, it would be possible for them to bring proceedings against those responsible for the tort (civil wrong) of 'nuisance'. The court might then ban the call to prayer by means of an order known as an 'injunction'. The local authority also has the right to serve a notice upon those responsible ordering them to refrain from causing a nuisance through excessive noise. Failure to comply with such a notice without reasonable excuse is a criminal offence under the Control of Pollution Act 1974.

For purposes of illustration a comparison can be made with the noise made by Christian practices. In two cases in the middle of the 19th century, local inhabitants complained about what they considered excessive noise being made by the ringing of church bells nearby. In the first case in 1851 the plaintiff objected to the frequent ringing of the bells of a Roman Catholic chapel in Clapham which had been established in the house next door to his. The bells were exceptionally large and heavy, made a tremendous noise and were rung five times a day, starting at 5.00 a.m., on weekdays and more often at weekends. Each ringing lasted 5-10 minutes. The court granted the plaintiff an 'injunction' ordering the defendant not to ring the bells in future in any way which would cause a nuisance or disturbance to the plaintiff.

In the second case in 1866 the Court refused to grant the plaintiff such an injunction to stop the tolling of church bells and the chiming of a church clock in Norbiton. The noise being made was considered insufficient to amount to a nuisance and was no more than a mere annoyance. Much therefore depends upon the scale of the noise being made in 'nuisance' cases.

2 REGISTRATION OF PLACES OF WORSHIP

Places of worship can be registered under the Places of Worship Registration Act 1855. This is not compulsory but there are certain advantages in doing so, as follows —

(a) Use for weddings

The building can also subsequently be registered under the Marriage Act 1949 so that ceremonies of marriage can lawfully be held there. As explained earlier (page 8) the building needs to be a 'separate' one in the sense that the whole of it is used as a place of worship. For registration under the Marriage Act to be achieved all that is required is a certificate signed by at least twenty house-holders stating that the building is being used by them as their usual place of public worship and that they desire registration for the purpose of having weddings celebrated there.

(b) Exemption from liability for rates

Local rates are not payable in respect of registered places of worship so long as they are available for 'public' worship. This means that 'the public at large' must be free to worship there, provided, of course, that they are prepared to behave in a reverent fashion and conform with the requirements of the religion concerned in matters of suitable dress etc. If only a select or exclusive group are allowed to worship there the building will not qualify for the exemption from liability. A Hindu temple, for example, which excluded a particular group of persons (eg 'untouchables') in a discriminatory way might well find that the exemption was not available. In those situations when the exemption does apply, it covers not only the place of worship itself but also any hall or similar building used in connection with the place of worship (eg for social or welfare activities) by the organisation responsible for the conduct of religious worship.

(c) Exemption from need for registration under the Charities Act

A religious building registered under the Places of Worship Act 1855 does not have to be registered under the Charities Act 1960. It is thus free from the system of control and supervision exercised by the Charities Commission.

(d) Protection against disturbance of worship

A building registered under the 1855 Act falls under the protection of the Ecclesiastical Courts Jurisdiction Act 1860. This means that any person guilty of riotous, violent or indecent behaviour there, whether or not during the celebration of worship, can be punished under the provisions of the Act. Perpetrators of such behaviour may also be punished under the Public Order legislation. In 1980 two white youths were fined for placing the head of a pig in a mosque at Batley Carr in Yorkshire while a group of Muslims were present. Under the Public Order Act 1986 a person can be guilty of an offence if he uses insulting words or behaviour with the intention of provoking another to use violence or within the sight or hearing of someone who is likely to be caused harassment, alarm or distress thereby.

Wouldn't the people guilty of the incident at Batley Carr also be committing the crime of blasphemy?

No. It is true that one of the definitions of blasphemy given in the dictionary is 'contempt or indignity offered to God', but the legal definition of the crime of blasphemy is much more limited. In one case a judge summed up the essence of the crime as being 'publication of any writing concerning God or Christ, the Christian religion, the Bible, or some sacred subject, using words which are scurrilous, abusive or offensive *and which tend to vilify the Christian religion*'. Many people, including the distinguished former judge, Lord Scarman, have criticised the fact that in legal terms blasphemy is confined to attacks upon the Christian religion. In a judgment in 1979 he commented that the definition of the crime was 'shackled by the chains of history' and declared —

> 'The offence belongs to a group of criminal offences designed to safeguard the internal tranquillity of the Kingdom. In an increasingly plural society such as that of modern Britain it is necessary not only to respect the differing religious beliefs, feelings and practices of all but to protect them from scurrility, vilification, ridicule and contempt.'

The question of whether or not the law needed to be changed was then referred by the Lord Chancellor to the Law Commission, a body which often recommends legal reforms. However, in 1985 it decided by a narrow majority (of three votes to two) to propose that the offence of blasphemy be abolished altogether rather than extended to faiths other than Christianity. This solution to the problem did not appeal to the Church of England or the British Government and so no steps were taken in Parliament to alter the law. However, during 1988 a committee set up by the Archbishop of Canterbury did recommend extension of the offence to other faiths in line with the views of the minority of the Law Commission. Later that year Salman Rushdie's book *The Satanic Verses* was published by Viking Penguin. Many British Muslims were gravely offended by passages in the book which they considered to be insulting towards Islam and the Prophet Mohammed. They protested to the Home Secretary and pleaded unsuccessfully with the publishers to withdraw the book. Early in 1989 Muslims in Bradford burnt a copy of the work in public to demonstrate their anger and their frustration at no prosecution being brought for blasphemy by the Crown Prosecution Service. Following deaths in Pakistan during demonstrations against the book, Ayatollah Khomeini pronounced a death sentence upon Salman Rushdie in February 1989. The British Government withdrew its diplomats from Iran in protest and indicated to a delegation of British Muslims that it had no intention of extending the blasphemy law to protect Islam as well as Christianity.

Mention was made earlier of Britain's commitment to the principle of freedom of religion under international human rights treaties. However, these treaties also guarantee freedom of expression and many non-Muslims in England took Salman Rushdie's side in the affair because they felt that authors should be free to write what they wanted. Even so, it is clear that there are many restrictions which can quite properly be placed upon freedom of expression under English law, eg to protect a person's reputation, to prohibit obscenity, to safeguard confidential information and to preserve the security of the state. Indeed it seemed rather curious that Sir Geoffrey Howe, then the British Foreign Secretary, should have stated in defence of Salman Rushdie that it was not the tradition in Britain for books to be 'banned', when the British Government had earlier taken such extensive measures to try to prevent publication of Peter Wright's book of memoirs, *Spycatcher*. The difficult issue at stake in the Rushdie affair was whether freedom of expression should take precedence over freedom of religion or vice-versa. Of course, if the English law of blasphemy had been altered before 1988 in order to protect Islam and the feelings of Muslims, it is highly likely that Viking Penguin's legal advisers would have forced Salman Rushdie to delete from his manuscript the passages which have gravely offended Muslims and so the book would never have been published in its present form.

How is registration of a place of worship under the 1855 Act actually achieved?

The first step is for the place to be 'certified' in writing in the form set out by the Act. This merely involves someone declaring in a document that the building is intended to be used as a place of meeting for religious worship by a congregation or assembly of persons, together with a reference to the name of their denomination or sect (if desired). Anyone may sign the form such as the owner or occupier of the building, a minister of religion or simply someone who has been attending worship there. The certificate has to be delivered in duplicate to the Superintendent Registrar of births, marriages and deaths in the district in which the building is situated and then sent on by him to the Registrar General. If the Registrar General is satisfied that the place mentioned is wholly or principally used as a place of meeting for religious worship and that the congregation is an identifiable and settled group, he will issue a certificate of registration through the Superintendent Registrar to the original certifying person. He will also note the date of registration in his records. There is no reason why a part of a building should not be so registered, eg a room in a private house which is set aside for worship by the group. The Registrar General's records suggest that only a relatively small percentage of the mosques, temples and *gurdwaras* in England have so far been registered under the Act.

3   BURIAL AND CREMATION

The normal methods of disposing of the dead depend largely upon differences between the various religious faiths. Muslims bury their dead (as do most Parsees today) whereas Hindus, Sikhs and Buddhists generally practise cremation. Sometimes members of the Asian communities may decide to send the bodies of deceased relatives back to their countries of origin, but normally burial or cremation is arranged in the UK and this section examines the English legal provisions on the matter.

(a) Burial

The vast majority of cemeteries in England are owned and maintained by a local authority. There are only a few cemeteries which are privately owned and of these perhaps the best known is the Brookwood Cemetery near Woking in Surrey. It spans 320 acres and is one of the largest in Western Europe. Originally opened in 1854, it has had separate facilities for Muslims for well over 100 years. Today it mainly caters for Muslim burials and serves much of southern England. There is also a privately owned Muslim cemetery in Nottingham.

Many local authorities have recently come to appreciate the desire of Muslims to have a separate area or section of their cemeteries set apart for Muslim burials and have managed to accommodate these wishes. In 1986 the Centre for the Study of Islam and Christian-Muslim Relations in Birmingham published a list of 56 local authorities which provided separate facilities for Muslim burials. The list is given below, with the location of the particular Muslim burial ground in brackets, where this is known.

Aylesbury
Barnet (Hendon)
Blackburn (Blackburn and Darwen)
Birmingham (Brandwood End
& Handsworth
Bolton
Bradford
Brent (Carpenders Park)
Bristol (Avon View)
Burnley
Bury
Calderdale (Elland)
Cambridge
Cardiff
Charnwood (Loughborough)
Chiltern
Coventry
Crawley
Derby
Ealing
East Staffs (Burton on Trent)
Gillingham
Gravesham
Hounslow (Hatton)
Hyndburn (Accrington)
Kirklees (Batley & Dewsbury)
Lambeth
Leicester (Saffron Hill)
Middlesborough (Thorntree)

Newport
Northampton (Towcester Road)
North Bedfordshire
Oxford (Botley)
Pendle (Wheatley Lane)
Peterborough (East Field)
Preston
Reading
Rochdale
Rochester (Chatham)
Rosendale (Haslingden)
Rugby (Croop Hill)
St Albans (London Road)
Sandwell (West Bromwich)
Sheffield
Slough
Southampton (Hollybrook)
Stoke on Trent
Tameside (Ashton-under-Lyne
and Hyde)
Walsall (Darlaston)
Waltham Forest
Wandsworth (Morden)
Warwick (Leamington)
Waverley (Farnham)
Wellingborough
Windsor and Maidenhead
Wolverhampton
Wycombe

121

Can a local authority be compelled to establish a separate public graveyard for Muslims?

It is doubtful whether local authorities are under a legal obligation to do this, although they might well be in breach of the Race Relations Act 1976 if they refused to do so while at the same time permitting other faiths to have separate facilities. Fortunately, a large number of those with substantial Muslim populations have responded positively to Muslim demands as the list above shows. Local authorities may also build and maintain prayer houses or 'chapels' in their cemeteries, which may be either non-denominational (and available for use by members of all faiths) or denominational (devoted to one faith). Denominational buildings have to be funded by the faith concerned, whereas those which are non-denominational can be financed out of local authority revenue.

How quickly can a burial be arranged in England?

Many Muslims consider that ideally a burial should be completed within 24 hours of death, but this is usually not possible in a public cemetery. Most local authorities require at least 48 hours' notice (excluding weekends and public holidays) and do not permit burials to take place at weekends or on public holidays. The need for speedy burial is perhaps not so pressing in the UK as in countries with hotter climates. Burials within 24 hours of death can always be arranged with the privately owned Brookwood Cemetery near Woking, and Blackburn and Preston are two examples of local authority cemeteries where burials are allowed at weekends and on public holidays.

Can the legal authorities delay a burial in order to allow a post-mortem examination to be conducted?

Yes, but this 'desecration of the body' offends the feelings of many people (including Muslims) and is only done where it is considered necessary. Under the Coroners Act 1887 an inquest can be held where, for example, there is a reasonable ground for suspecting that a person has died a violent or unnatural death or else has died suddenly of unknown causes. As part of the inquest proceedings the coroner is entitled to direct that a post-mortem examination be carried out.

Furthermore, under the Coroners (Amendment) Act 1926 where a coroner is informed that the dead body of a person is lying within his area of jurisdiction and there are reasonable grounds for suspecting that the person has died a sudden death of which the cause is unknown, if the coroner is of the opinion that a post-mortem examination may prove an inquest to be unnecessary he may similarly arrange for a post-mortem examination to be performed. Coroners also possess the power to order the 'exhumation' or digging up of a body where this is necessary for the holding of an inquest or for reasons connected with the institution of criminal proceedings in respect of a death.

Do local burial authorities allow Muslims to be buried so that their graves are aligned with Mecca?

Muslims generally believe that a grave should run from north-east to south-west so that the body can lie on its side and face towards Mecca, which is in a south-easterly direction. So far as is known no burial authority has refused to permit this, although it is unclear whether they are under any legal duty to do so.

Must a coffin be used for all burials in England?

There is no specific legal provision on this question and the matter is thus left to individual local authorities to decide. Most appear to object to burials without a coffin because they feel the practice may be unhygienic, but it is thought that there is little real substance in this objection. Some local authorities definitely do allow uncoffined burials, including Bradford, Kirklees, Blackburn, Newport, Waverley, and Windsor and Maidenhead, as does the private Brookwood Cemetery near Woking. Others are perfectly willing to allow the coffin to remain open right up to the time of burial so that the mourners can take a final look at the deceased before the body is lowered into the grave and also ensure that the deceased's face is correctly turned towards Mecca.

Do local authorities respect the wishes of Muslims that graves should be raised a few inches from the ground so that they are clearly visible and will not be desecrated by people walking over them by mistake?

Unfortunately this question does present some difficulties. Following a burial it is normal practice for the gravediggers to build a small mound of earth over the grave. However, this usually subsides within a comparatively short time, as rain falls, and eventually the ground will be reasonably level. Most local authorities prefer the surface to be as flat as possible so as to allow the grass growing on top to be cut easily by a lawnmower. Under the Local Authorities Cemeteries Order 1977 local authorities are entitled to maintain the surfaces of graves at the same level as the adjoining ground and they also have the right to refuse permission for any memorial stones to be laid on top of graves. Some enforce this right quite strictly and bar 'kerbs', border stones and other surroundings (such as fencing or railings). They only allow headstones to be erected. It seems sad that they should place a higher value upon the ease of maintaining cemeteries in a tidy condition than upon respecting the religious traditions and wishes of mourners. Anyone who feels strongly about this should investigate the question with a number of conveniently situated local authorities (to see if they have different rules) and also consider carefully whether it would not be wiser to arrange for a burial to take place in a private cemetery, where the religious requirements will be properly observed and kerbs and borders are permitted as well as a headstone.

(b) Cremation

Cremation is a relatively modern phenomenon in England and it was not until the beginning of this century that Parliament passed legislation to confer formal approval upon the practice and regulate the process. The important statutes are now the Cremation Acts 1902 and 1952.

The first crematorium was established at Woking in 1878 and since then the popularity of cremation among the white community has grown steadily, so that today the proportion of cremations to burials is 70:30. Crematoria may be operated either privately or by local authorities.

No cremation may occur unless an application has been made for it, on a prescribed form, usually by the nearest relative of the deceased or by the executor of his or her will. If the deceased had expressed a wish, either to be cremated or not to be, this wish would naturally normally be honoured and carried out, but in law it is not strictly binding on the deceased's relations or executors, who are entitled to choose between cremation and burial. No cremation is allowed to take place without *either* two medical certificates from different medical practitioners as to the cause of death *or* a post-mortem examination *or* a coroner's inquest.

After the cremation has occurred the ashes must be delivered to the person who applied for the cremation, if he or she so desires, and that person is then free to decide whether to keep them or how to dispose of them. Otherwise the cremation authority will dispose of them.

Is there any legal objection to the scattering of human ashes in an English river?

In India it is common practice for the ashes to be consigned to one of the many holy rivers, the holiest of all being the Ganges. Varanasi (formerly Benares) is often the preferred location for the disposal of the remains of the departed and there are funeral pyres in continual operation on the river bank. Although there are no 'holy' rivers in England, many Hindus (and Sikhs) wish to consign the cremated remains of their relations to flowing waters here, in accordance with their religious beliefs and traditions. This has given rise to some concern on the part of certain sections of the majority community, who have expressed objections both on aesthetic grounds and on the basis that there might be a risk to public health. Attention is sometimes drawn by such objectors to the fact that the Indian Government is presently undertaking a massive 'Action Plan' to clean up the River Ganges and it is argued that this provides strong evidence of the need to prevent the pollution of English rivers which might arise from the disposal of human ashes in them. However, the pollution of the Ganges is largely caused by the discharge of untreated sewage and the deposit of industrial waste, as well as by the fact that partly charred corpses are disposed of there. In the case of young children and those too poor to afford to buy wood for a funeral pyre, uncremated corpses are also deposited in the river. This is a very different situation from the scattering of a very small quantity of ashes following a cremation in an English crematorium. In many cases Hindus and Sikhs living in England do in fact send the ashes back to India for disposal there, but this may prove too expensive for the poorer members of these communities.

In a number of instances where Hindus and Sikhs have raised the question of scattering ashes in English rivers with their local water authorities, the response has been that this would be unacceptable. This was the attitude taken by the Severn-Trent Water Authority in the West Midlands in 1981-82 and by the Anglian Water Authority in the Bedford area during 1985-86. The Authorities had to take into account not only the adverse reactions of local white residents but also the provisions of the Control of Pollution Act 1974. This Act made it a criminal offence to permit (i) 'any poisonous, noxious or polluting matter' and (ii) 'any solid waste matter' to enter any stream, river or watercourse. These provisions are now to be found in the Water Act 1989. Although category (i) above may well not be applicable to this question because the exact definition of 'polluting matter' is unclear and has never been decided by an English court, it seems likely that human ashes do fall into category (ii). Since the quantity of ashes amounting from a single cremation is so small, it seems improbable that anyone would actually be prosecuted for scattering them in a river, especially in view of the far more harmful substances which the law and the water authorities allow to be discharged there. However, for anyone who wishes to be clearly on the right side of English law there is a reasonably satisfactory alternative, at least for those who live quite close to the sea. The Water Act 1989 expressly provides that no offence is committed if a person has been granted a licence to deposit ashes under the Food and Environment Protection Act 1985. Such licences can easily be obtained from the District Fisheries Inspectors of the Ministry of Agriculture, Fisheries and Food (for the addresses of such Inspectors contact the Ministry at Great Westminster House, Horseferry Road, London SW1P 2AE; tel: 01-216 6311). The Ministry can, however, only issue licences in respect of disposals in tidal or estuary waters (or in the sea within 12 miles of the coastline), and not in inland waters or freshwater. Even so, this means that it is perfectly possible to dispose of ashes in, for example, the Lower River Trent (at Humberside) and the Lower River Severn (in the Bristol Channel), ie below the tidal limits, and local boatmen are available to assist in making such arrangements. The District Fisheries Inspector issues the licence in the form of a simple letter authorising the disposal on a particular day at a particular place. Both ashes and corpses (suitably weighted down) can be disposed of lawfully in this manner.

4 SWEARING OATHS IN COURT PROCEEDINGS

A person who gives evidence in court, either in a case in which he or she is one of the parties to the litigation or in proceedings between other people, may be asked to give this evidence on oath. A Christian swears such an oath on the New Testament and declares —

> 'I swear by Almighty God that I shall speak the truth, the whole truth and nothing but the truth'.

In the 17th century there was a vigorous dispute between two very distinguished English lawyers, Lord Coke and Sir Matthew Hale, as to whether non-Christian witnesses could give evidence at all in the English courts. It was Hale's view that they could which eventually triumphed. In the case of *Fachina v Sabine* in 1738 a Muslim gave evidence after being sworn on the *Quran*, and in the case of *Omychund v Barker* in 1744 it was decided that the evidence of a number of Hindu witnesses given in Calcutta could be properly admitted by an English court. They had been solemnly sworn in accordance with what appeared to be the practice in Calcutta at that time, namely by touching the *brahmin's* hand or foot.

The current law is contained in the Oaths Act 1978 which allows persons of every religious faith to take an oath in whatever manner the particular faith provides. Muslims usually swear on the *Quran*, Hindus may swear on the *Bhagavad Gita* or the *Vedas*, Sikhs may swear on the *Guru Granth Sahib* or *Gutka* and Parsees may swear on the *Zendavesta*. Buddhist oaths have been recognised by the English courts and a particularly odd form (or distortion) of a Chinese oath, involving the witness in smashing a saucer in the court, has also been allowed for Confucians.

What happens if it is discovered after the witness has given sworn evidence that he or she did not have any religious beliefs?

It makes no difference. The oath is treated as valid. The same applies if the oath was administered wrongly. The evidence remains valid.

Do all witnesses have to take an oath in one form or another?

No, there is an alternative. A witness may choose instead to make a 'solemn affirmation'. When the court official asks the witness to take an oath the witness is perfectly entitled to object and refuse, without the need to give any reason. Some Hindus, Sikhs and Chinese do not wish to swear oaths and they should ask to make a solemn affirmation instead. Quaker witnesses have been allowed to do this since the 17th century and this right now extends to everyone, regardless of whether or not they have any religious beliefs.

Do the courts attach greater significance to evidence given on oath than to evidence given by a witness who has made a solemn affirmation?

No, they treat both types of evidence as equally valuable. Witnesses who deliberately give false evidence will be guilty of the crime of perjury regardless of whether they have sworn or solemnly affirmed.

What is the position if a Muslim witness wishes to swear on oath but the court does not possess a copy of the *Quran*?

If a copy can be obtained reasonably quickly from somewhere else the court may agree to a delay to enable this to be done. Otherwise the court can decide that in view of the inconvenience involved, the witness should solemnly affirm instead. The same practice is adopted with adherents to other faiths whose holy books are not easily available.

CHAPTER 14

The criminal law

1 THE QUESTION OF GUILT

For a long time the general approach of the English courts has been to apply a uniform and consistent standard to all those who are accused of criminal offences, regardless of whether or not they have foreign origins. The purpose of the criminal law is to impose certain minimum standards of behaviour which the community as a whole regards as necessary for the peaceful order of society. It is therefore logical to apply, in the vast majority of circumstances, a universal set of principles to determine who is guilty and who is innocent.

In a case in 1852 involving French defendants who were on a murder charge the judge stated —

'To make a difference in the case of foreigners would be a most dangerous practice. It is of great importance that the administration of the law should be uniform. It must be administered without respect to persons [ie without favouring particular people], and it would be dangerous and unjust to introduce into a general rule an exception in favour of foreigners.'

This general principle of uniformity will thus apply to most crimes, such as offences against persons (including murder, assault, kidnapping, carrying offensive weapons and sexual offences) and offences against property (such as burglary and theft). It also applies to offences such as corruption and the misuse of drugs.

The fact that the accused was ignorant of the rules of English law will not afford any defence, nor will it be relevant that the conduct in question would have been perfectly lawful if it had occurred in the accused's country of origin.

For example, female circumcision and the tattooing of children are both lawful in parts of Asia but they are statutory offences under English law.

Two cases may be described to illustrate the application of the basic rule about guilt. In *R v Ahmed Shah Moied* (1987) each of the accused had organised or participated in the abduction and detention of a 20 year old girl, Zahida. She had left the family home in Southampton to study in Chelmsford and had formed an association with a white youth. The girl's father had thereupon sought the advice of a local community leader of Pakistani origin as to what steps to take and he had then recruited a private detective to snatch the girl from her lodgings. All three of them were found guilty on charges of kidnapping or 'false imprisonment' (wrongful detention).

In *R v Husseyin Ozdemir* (1986) a police officer had caught the accused's son (aged 14) driving a car and had indicated to the accused that the son would be charged with an offence for driving without a licence. The father, who owned a Turkish restaurant, responded by offering the policeman £50 if he would forget about the case. When that failed he said —

'Please, he's my son, if you want to you can come to my restaurant with your girlfriend and you can have a free meal any time.'

The police officer reported this incident to his senior officers and the accused was charged with corruption. He was convicted and sentenced to a short term of imprisonment.

Would a Sikh who carried a *kirpan* (religious dagger) be guilty of possession of a dangerous weapon?

The *kirpan* is recognised as one of the five distinctive symbols of Sikhism and the carrying of *kirpans* is expressly recognised as lawful by the Indian Constitution, so it is hardly likely that the mere act of carrying one in England would amount to a criminal offence. The Criminal Justice Act 1988 which contains provisions designed to penalise those who carry knives and other sharply pointed articles specifically states that it is a defence for an accused to prove that he had the article with him in a public place for 'religious reasons'. Of course, if it were proved that a Sikh was carrying a *kirpan* in a public place with the intention of attacking another person, a criminal offence would have been committed. The accused would be guilty of being in possession of an 'offensive weapon' under the Prevention of Crime Act 1969.

Would a Muslim who married two wives in England be guilty of the crime of bigamy?

Yes. It would be no defence for him to argue that under Muslim law he was entitled to have up to four wives at the same time. Polygamy is not permitted in England. However, if his first marriage took place outside the UK in a country where polygamy was permitted and if it was recognised as valid in the eyes of English law, then it would not be bigamy for him to marry a second wife in England. The second 'marriage' would be 'void' and ineffective but no criminal charges would follow. This is because the English courts have decided that the crime of bigamy depends upon the first marriage being a monogamous one in legal terms.

What would be the position if a Muslim married his first wife in England and his second wife in, say, Pakistan?

Since the first marriage was monogamous in the eyes of English law a charge of bigamy might be brought if the husband later returned to England. However, the law is unclear on this point and there is no reported case in which such a prosecution has been attempted.

2 THE DISCRETION TO PROSECUTE

Most prosecutions are now decided upon by the Crown Prosecution Service, whereas formerly most were laid by the police. The prosecuting authorities have a discretion as to whether or not to press charges in any particular case. Sometimes they may consider that they only need to 'caution' an offender and warn him not to repeat the action concerned. There are many factors which the authorities are entitled to take into account in reaching their decision, such as the chances of the suspect being convicted and whether the breach of the law was of merely a trivial or technical nature. 'Cautions' are now quite common in cases where people are in breach of the Misuse of Drugs Act 1971 through merely possessing very small quantities of cannabis for their own personal use. However, anyone caught importing or supplying large quantities of the drug to others will invariably be prosecuted. Possession of certain other more danger-ous drugs such as cocaine and heroin is very likely to result in prosecution. *Kat* (or *ghat*), sometimes known as 'Arabian tea' and widely chewed in the Middle East and East Africa is not, however, on the banned list and may be freely imported and used in Britain.

3   THE PROCESS OF SENTENCING

Once an accused person has been convicted of an offence, the court has to decide upon the appropriate punishment or sentence. There are a variety of choices open to the court including fines, probation and 'community service orders', as well as committal to a period of imprisonment. Many factors have to be considered including the gravity of the crime, the harm done and the circumstances and personality of the defendant. When the question of sentence (as opposed to the issue of guilt) arises, it is right and proper that the court should be made aware of such matters as the defendant's foreign origins, ignorance of English law, adherence to ethnic or religious customs and traditions, and difficulty in adjusting to English standards of behaviour. Any of these matters may serve as 'mitigating circumstances' reducing the defendant's moral responsibility and thus calling for a degree of leniency in fixing the appropriate sentence.

A good example of such leniency being shown is provided by the case of *R v Bashir Begum Bibi* (1980). The defendant was a Kenyan Asian widow, aged 48, who had been found guilty of being involved in the import of cannabis, contrary to the Misuse of Drugs Act 1971. During the proceedings the report of a social worker revealed that she had been totally dependent for her support and welfare on her brother-in-law. It was he who had organised the illegal importing of the drugs and he had already been convicted and sentenced to three and a half years' imprisonment. The widow had merely unpacked the parcels of cannabis when they arrived at her home from Kenya and she was clearly only on the fringes of the enterprise. She was so well socialised into the Muslim traditions of *purdah* and male dominance that the Court felt it was unlikely that she really appreciated the significance of what she had done. She had had no contact with wider English society and her involvement in the offence appeared to arise out of a normal response of simply accepting the decisions made by her male relations. The sentence of three years' imprisonment imposed upon her by the Crown Court was therefore reduced by the Court of Appeal to one of six months. This was felt to be more appropriate for both the offence and the offender and it meant her immediate release from the gaol where she had already spent six months in custody.

A further illustration of a lenient sentence being imposed by the court is the case of *R v Sughran Bibi* (1989). The defendant had been ordered to attend at Leeds Crown Court to give evidence for the prosecution in a fraud trial. Her husband told her not to attend and as a result the trial was impeded. The judge held that this amounted to 'contempt of court' and that she could not rely on her duty to obey her husband as a defence. Instead she had to obey English law. However, in choosing the appropriate sentence to pass he took account of her cultural background and fined her £250. The judge expressly stated that if she had been a member of the majority community he would have been much more severe and almost certainly sent her to prison.

4 SPECIFIC RELIGIOUS EXEMPTIONS

In three specific areas Parliament has created exemptions from liability under the general criminal law in order to accommodate the religious practices of minority groups. This means that only members of the religious community concerned are free from criminal responsibility; others will still be guilty of the relevant offence.

(a) Motorcyclists and crash helmets

Regulations made by the Minister of Transport under the Road Traffic Act 1972 require motorcyclists to wear helmets complying with high safety standards. Failure to do so is a criminal offence. Following a vigorous public campaign by Sikhs and their supporters, Parliament passed legislation in 1976 to accommodate the needs of those Sikhs who wear turbans. The Motor-Cycle Crash Helmets (Religious Exemption) Act 1976 provides that any requirement imposed now or later by regulations under the 1972 Act shall not apply to any follower of the Sikh religion 'while he is wearing a turban'. It should be noted that the exemption clearly only protects turbanned Sikhs. Anyone else riding a motorcycle without a helmet is guilty of an offence.

(b) The slaughter of animals and poultry

The general law, as laid down in the Slaughterhouses Act 1974, is that a standard practice must be followed when animals are slaughtered in a slaughterhouse or abattoir. This practice involves 'stunning' the animal so that it is insensible to pain, before actually killing it. Cattle, sheep and goats are included among the animals to which the rule applies and similar provisions are contained in the Slaughter of Poultry Act 1967 affecting turkeys, chickens and other domestic fowl. The purpose of the legislation is to ensure that as little pain and suffering as possible is caused and anyone contravening the Acts is guilty of a criminal offence. However, both Acts contain an exemption for Muslims and Jews, to enable them to comply with their religious laws and traditions in this area. So far as Muslims are concerned, the normal method of slaughtering is known as *dhabh* and it involves cutting the throat of the animal or fowl while it is still conscious so as to allow the blood to start flowing out while it is still alive. It is true that some Muslim slaughterhouses have used the pre-stunning method in the UK on the basis of permission granted by the local *imam*, but they appear

---

to be in the minority. The meat produced by the religious method of slaughter is known as *halal* and strict Muslims will only eat meat prepared in this manner. In order to comply with the law, *dhabh* must be performed both by a Muslim and for the food of Muslims. In the case of *Malins v Cole and Attard* (1986) a Muslim slaughterman was convicted of an offence under the Slaughter of Poultry Act because the chicken he was caught selling in the Petticoat Lane market area of London's East End had not been slaughtered for the food of Muslims. It had been bought by and slaughtered for a man wearing a crucifix (who later turned out to be an RSPCA inspector) without any check having been made by the slaughterman that it would in fact be used for the food of Muslims, as the statute requires.

Some Muslim shopkeepers and grocers are known to slaughter chickens on their premises without these premises being licensed as an abattoir and without the necessary planning permission. In so doing they are clearly committing offences and are liable to be fined. Sometimes they have sought to justify their conduct on the grounds that their customers like to ensure that the *dhabh* method is being properly followed (including recitation of a prayer before the slaughter of each bird) by watching the kill themselves, rather than purchasing from a large abattoir with a production line where the ritual prayer might be omitted in the interests of greater productivity. However, the law is well established and the solution is for these abattoirs to be inspected by the customers (or their religious leaders) rather than for shops in mainly residential areas to violate the planning laws. In two cases, *Hussain v Secretary of State for the Environment* (1971) and *Ahmed v Department of the Environment* (1972) the courts ruled that the keeping and slaughtering of poultry is not a use 'ordinarily incidental' to the running of a retail shop and therefore specific planning permission is needed. Detailed hygiene requirements need to be satisfied because of the risks to health from such an activity. These are contained in the Food Hygiene (General) Regulations 1970 and the Poultry Meat (Hygiene) Regulations 1976.

If an animal (or a fowl) is to be slaughtered for food other than at an abattoir (eg it is planned to slaughter a sheep or goat at home to celebrate a festival) the provisions of the Protection of Animals Act 1911 apply and here there is no special religious exemption. The main rules are first, that no unnecessary suffering must be inflicted upon the animal and secondly, no 'operation' must be performed on the animal 'without due care and humanity'. In a case in 1984 a Cypriot was fined £200 by a magistrates' court following his conviction under the Act for slaughtering three goats at his home by cutting their throats.

(c) **Sunday trading**

Although it is subject to numerous exceptions, of which most traders are very well aware, the Shops Act 1950 contains a general ban on shops being open on Sundays. Since 1950 many attempts have been made in Parliament either to legalise Sunday trading completely or else at least to extend and rationalise the exceptions, but so far all have failed. However, shopkeepers of the Jewish faith can obtain an exemption from the prohibition on Sunday trading by registering with the local authority and closing their shops on Saturdays so as to enable them to observe the Jewish Sabbath.

5 **MEDICAL MATTERS**

A variety of medical matters are regulated by the criminal law with a view to protecting patients from harm and prohibiting certain practices which are not felt to be in the public interest.

(a) **The practice of Asian medicine**

Many Asians in England make considerable use of traditional medicine, either in preference to modern medicine or when it fails to cure their illnesses. *Hakims, vaids* and acupuncturists are to be found in many English towns and cities. They have extensive practices and treat patients both by seeing them in person and by dealing with postal inquiries. They sometimes make very grand claims for the effectiveness of their herbal and other remedies in advertisements in the Asian press.

Are traditional medical practitioners allowed to describe themselves as 'doctors' in England?

No. Under the Medical Act 1983 only properly qualified and registered medical practitioners are entitled to use words such as 'doctor of medicine', 'physician', 'surgeon' or 'general practitioner'. Others who do so are liable to be charged with a criminal offence and fined. It is, however, a defence for the accused to prove that he honestly believed he was permitted to use one of these titles, for instance because he had obtained some medical qualifications overseas.

Do traditional healers have to obtain any form of licence to practise?

No, there is no system for licensing or registering them. Such a system would probably be a good idea so that some check could be made upon their skill and competence. Apparently there are many practising in England who would not be allowed to do so in the Indian subcontinent because they have no qualifica-

135

tions. Unlike registered doctors, traditional healers are not obliged by law to carry insurance against claims for negligence. Hence, if their advice or treatment itself causes injury or illness, the patient may bring a successful claim for compensation only to discover later that the healer does not have enough money to satisfy the amount ordered by the court.

Are any Asian medicines banned because they have been found to be dangerous to health?

The Department of Health has power to ban the supply, sale and import of medicinal products in the interests of health and safety and various Asian remedies have been found to contain dangerous substances such as lead, mercury and arsenic. The baby herbal tonic *Bal Jivan Chamcho* was banned in 1977 because it was found to have a lead-contaminated spoon.

The medicine and cosmetic known as *surma*, which is applied to the eyes, has also been found to have high concentrations of lead in it and the government have issued public warnings about its use as well as prohibiting its sale within the UK. In one case a boy of four from Oldham was thought to have died as a result of lead poisoning from *surma* and many Asian children are still being admitted to hospital after its application.

Are traditional healers breaking the law if they make false claims in advertisements about the effectiveness of their remedies?

Yes. The Medicines Act 1968 provides that those who manufacture, sell or supply medicines are guilty of an offence if they issue 'false or misleading advertisements' about medicinal products. Some traditional practitioners do make some very extravagant claims for their products in the Asian press and they are liable to prosecution if they break the terms of the Act. Furthermore, a person who, in the course of a trade or business, applies a false trade description to any goods or supplies any goods to which a false trade description is applied, can be charged with a criminal offence under the Trade Descriptions Act 1968.

(b) 'Selective' abortion

According to various media reports some pregnant Asian women in England have sought abortions in recent years upon discovering (via medical tests designed to check whether the foetus is healthy and normal) that they are carrying girls rather than boys. Such a request for an abortion is normally motivated by the family's desire to have a son and heir as the next child, often in cases where all the children so far have been girls. This practice has been going on for several years in India where among the Hindu community the birth of a son has particular religious significance. A son is needed to perform the funeral rites for his father and a Hindu can only attain salvation after death (and ensure that of his ancestors too) if offerings are made to the deities by a son or grandson etc., down the line of legitimate male issue. A son's offerings guarantee bliss for the spirit of the departed, whereas heaven is closed to those without male progeny. Another reason, of course, for preferring male children is economic. Parents are often anxious about their capacity to provide substantial dowries for their daughters upon their marriages. This can cause them considerable strain, especially in the light of the ill-treatment of brides whose families are felt to have fallen short of the degree of generosity expected by the husband's relatives.

The performance of an abortion in England upon the specific and sole ground of the sex of the foetus would clearly be unlawful. It would involve a contravention of the Abortion Act 1967 and would render the clinic, the doctor and the woman concerned liable to criminal charges. The Act provides that abortions are only allowed where two registered medical practitioners have formed the opinion, in good faith, that one of the following grounds exists, namely —

(i)   that the continuation of the pregnancy would involve a greater risk to the life of the pregnant woman, or of injury to the physical or mental health of the pregnant woman or any existing children of her family, than any risk if the pregnancy were terminated;

   or

(ii) that there is a substantial risk that if the child were born it would suffer from such physical or mental abnormalities as to be seriously handicapped.

In determining whether the continuation of a pregnancy would involve risk or injury to the pregnant woman's health in (i) above, account may be taken of her actual or reasonably foreseeable environment. This makes it possible for an abortion to be carried out quite lawfully upon what are commonly referred to as 'social' or 'economic' grounds.

Hence, provided the reason given to the doctor is related to these grounds, for example that the family already has three daughters and will not be able to cope adequately with a further daughter or that the birth of a girl will expose the mother to considerable hostility from the father through physical violence or emotional cruelty, some doctors are perfectly willing to perform an abortion and are unlikely to be in any serious danger of breaking the law. Many thousands of white women in England who do not want to proceed with their pregnancies for a variety of social and economic reasons relating to their ages, family circumstances, educational programmes and career plans, are able to obtain lawful abortions every year.

However, in the light of public concern about the propriety of pre-natal tests used exclusively for determining sex, it is likely that such tests will be discontinued in England. The correct (and very valuable) use of pre-natal tests is to try to detect hereditary diseases.

(c) **Surrogate motherhood**

The desire of Asian families to have a male heir (which, as we have just seen, motivates some women to request abortions of female children) may also lead to the use of the techniques of surrogacy. A married couple who are unable to have children may seek to solve the problem by arranging with another couple who are relations or close friends, for the transfer of a child specially conceived for the purpose. An agreement is reached whereby this child will be handed over to the infertile couple (the 'commissioning parents') at birth and to all intents and purposes the child will thereafter be regarded as their own child. Such private, domestic surrogacy arrangements are viewed by many people as much more acceptable than commercial arrangements organised by agencies for profit. Accordingly it is only the commercial schemes which are currently outlawed by the Surrogacy Arrangements Act 1985 and which can lead to prosecutions being brought. This Act prohibits the negotiating of a surrogacy arrangement on a commercial basis, ie where payments are to be made or received in respect of the arrangement (other than a payment to the surrogate mother herself, which is allowed). However, even in commercial surrogacy cases neither the surrogate mother nor the commissioning couple are guilty of any offence — only the agency, and doctors and others who organise the arrangement. On the other hand, anyone (including the commissioning parents or a prospective surrogate mother) can be guilty of a different offence under the Act, namely the advertising of or for surrogacy arrangements, whether or not the surrogacy is to be on a commercial basis. Hence it is a crime to insert an advertisement in a newspaper or in a shop window indicating that an infertile couple are looking for a woman willing to become a surrogate mother.

In order for the commissioning parents to acquire full parental responsibility with respect to a child born to a surrogate mother, they will need to adopt the child through obtaining an order of the court. Generally it is a criminal offence under the Adoption Act 1976 for anyone to give or offer to give someone else money in return for the transfer of a child with a view to adoption. Hence, if the commissioning parents promise to compensate a surrogate mother for her expenses or loss of earnings in bearing the child, they might be guilty of an offence if the plan was for the commissioning parents to adopt the child later. However, in the case of *Re Adoption Application: Surrogacy* (1987) the Court ruled that such a payment could be made legally if it was done with the authorisation of the Court and this could even be done retrospectively. In that case the adoption was allowed because the surrogate mother agreed to it and the welfare of the child would be best served by being adopted by the commissioning parents.

6 THE RIGHTS OF PRISONERS

Under English law the theory is that prisoners only lose those of their civil rights which are explicitly taken away from them (such as their freedom of movement) or which are implicitly denied them as a result of their confinement (such as their freedom to choose a particular form of employment). Hence their right to freedom of religion, for example, is meant to remain unaffected. However, in practical terms there are bound to be many restrictions placed upon the activities of prisoners, if not upon their thoughts or beliefs. Even so, the prison authorities usually do try to do their best to accommodate many of the religious needs and cultural traditions of Asian prisoners and there are various legal provisions on the subject generally.

(a) Registration of religion

Under the Prison Act 1952 every prisoner is entitled to register his or her adherence to a particular religious faith upon entry into any prison. The prison governor is under a duty to record this information. In the unlikely event of a conversion to a different faith while in prison, the prisoner may apply to the 'board of visitors' to have the record amended and steps will be taken to do this unless there is reason to doubt that the prisoner is acting in good faith and to suspect that the alleged spiritual conversion is not a genuine one.

In 1986 the Prison Service issued a 'Race Relations Policy Statement' which contained the following declaration —

'Members of minority religious groups have the same right to practise their faith as those of the majority faith. Wherever feasible in prison circumstances arrangements are made to give them the same practical opportunity to do so.'

In February 1989 there were 1,819 Muslims, 469 Sikhs, 194 Hindus and 140 Buddhists in the 121 English and Welsh prison service establishments (ie prisons, detention centres, remand centres and youth custody centres).

(b) Worship

The Prison Act 1952 provides that where in any prison the number of prisoners who belong to a faith other than the Church of England is sufficiently large, in the view of the Home Secretary, as to require the appointment of a minister of the faith, the Home Secretary may appoint such a minister to that prison. Many such appointments have been made and as a result there are, for example, around 90 prison establishments where *imams* visit Muslim prisoners on a regular basis every week.

Where such an appointment is not justified because there are too few adherents, the Prison Commissioners may simply allow such a minister to visit prisoners of the particular faith concerned on a more informal basis. The prison governor must do what he reasonably can to arrange for regular visits by a minister in these circumstances if any prisoner requests him to do so. However, in some parts of the country it may prove difficult for him to obtain the services of a minister of the particular faith demanded because of lack of availability.

Prisoners from minority faiths normally have to meet for collective acts of worship either in Christian chapels or in secular accommodation such as classrooms, dining-rooms, libraries, offices, etc. Only in a very few prisons is specially designed accommodation available. Muslims are always allowed to meet together for congregational prayers in the middle of the day on Fridays.

(c) Festivals

Arrangements must be made by the prison authorities so as not to require prisoners to do any unnecessary work on their recognised days of religious observance. Thus Muslim prisoners are exempt from work on the days of *Eid-al-Fitr* and *Eid-al-Adha* and congregational prayers are organised on the mornings of each of these two days. Buddhist prisoners are not required to work on the festival of *Vesak*.

(d) Diet

It is only in very exceptional circumstances that prisons fail to respect the dietary restrictions of Muslims, Hindus and Sikhs. Vegetarian menus are almost always available and an increasing number of establishments are now able to offer Muslims *halal* meat on a regular basis. Most make special arrangements during the month of Ramadan so that sufficient food is supplied in the evenings for two meals, one of which can be eaten after sunset and the other before dawn the following day. In some prisons the practice has grown up of permitting the local *imam* to deliver food specially for the feasts of *Eid-al-Fitr* and *Eid-al-Adha*.

(e) Dress, religious articles and books

Normally, baptised Sikhs are allowed to wear the five 'Ks' together with their turbans, Muslims are permitted to keep caps and prayer-mats as personal possessions in their cells and Buddhists are entitled to use images of the Buddha. However, Sikhs are only allowed to wear a thin bangle (rather than a thick one with a sharp edge) and the *kirpan* must be a tiny replica (eg inlaid in a comb). Muslim women are permitted to wear clothes which cover their entire bodies and to keep their heads covered and Hindu women may wear saris. So far as is reasonably practicable every prisoner must have made available to him or her such religious books recognised by his or her faith as are approved by the Home Secretary.

Where are all these legal rules about prisoners' rights to be found?

Some of them are in the Prison Rules 1964 (and equivalent rules for youth custody centres and detention centres). Others are in various Circular Instructions issued to prison establishments by the Home Office. The latter are not made available to the general public so it is usually quite difficult for prisoners to know exactly what their 'rights' are. More importantly these 'rights' cannot normally be enforced by means of court proceedings. They are really no more than 'privileges' and if they are not provided, an individual prisoner's only remedy is to make a formal complaint to the governor if the prison staff fail to afford the facilities requested.

A useful *Directory and Guide on Religious Practices in H M Prison Service* was published by the Prison Service Chaplaincy in 1988. Inquiries should be addressed to the Assistant Chaplain General (M), Midland Regional HQ, Calthorpe House, Hagley Road, Birmingham B16 8QR (telephone: 021-455 9855).

Table of statutes referred to

143

Table of cases referred to

(For list of case report abbreviations, see page 148)

List of case report abbreviations

AC	Law Reports (Appeal Cases)
AIR	All India Reporter
All ER	All England Law Reports
CLY	Current Law Yearbook
Cr AR	Criminal Appeal Reports
Cr AR(S)	Criminal Appeal Reports (Sentencing)
ER	Employment Report (CRE)
Fam	Law Reports (Family Division)
Fam Law	Family Law
FLR	Family Law Reports
ICR	Industrial Cases Reports
IDS	International Data Services
Imm AR	Immigration Appeal Reports
INLP	Immigration and Nationality Law and Practice
IRLR	Industrial Relations Law Reports
P	Law Reports (Probate Division)
QB	Law Reports (Queen's Bench Division)
SJ	Solicitors' Journal
WLR	Weekly Law Reports

List of useful addresses

Commission for Racial Equality (CRE), Elliot House, 10/12 Allington Street, London SW1E 5EH (Tel: 01-828 7022)

Home Office (Immigration Dept), Lunar House, Wellesley Road, Croydon, CR9 2BY (Tel: 01-686 0688)

Indian Workers' Association, 112a The Green, Southall, Middlesex UB2 4BQ (Tel: 01-574 6019)

Joint Council for the Welfare of Immigrants (JCWI), 115 Old Street, London EC1V 9JR (Tel: 01-251 8706)

United Kingdom Immigrants Advisory Service (UKIAS), County House, 190 Great Dover Street, London SE1 4YB (Tel: 01-357 6917)

Index